To Susan,

Thank you for your friendship and support, Our best wishes

Salvaged by Love

A True Story of Love, Loss, and Love Found Again

HARVEY HOFF

BALBOA
PRESS

Balboa Press books may be ordered through booksellers or by contacting:

Balboa Press
A Division of Hay House
1663 Liberty Drive
Bloomington, IN 47403
www.balboapress.com
1 (877) 407-4847

Because of the dynamic nature of the Internet, any web addresses or
links contained in this book may have changed since publication and
may no longer be valid. The views expressed in this work are solely those
of the author and do not necessarily reflect the views of the publisher,
and the publisher hereby disclaims any responsibility for them.

The author of this book does not dispense medical advice or prescribe the use
of any technique as a form of treatment for physical, emotional, or medical
problems without the advice of a physician, either directly or indirectly. The
intent of the author is only to offer information of a general nature to help
you in your quest for emotional and spiritual well-being. In the event you use
any of the information in this book for yourself, which is your constitutional
right, the author and the publisher assume no responsibility for your actions.

Any people depicted in stock imagery provided by Thinkstock are models,
and such images are being used for illustrative purposes only.
Certain stock imagery © Thinkstock.

Print information available on the last page.

ISBN: 978-1-5043-9320-1 (sc)
ISBN: 978-1-5043-9322-5 (hc)
ISBN: 978-1-5043-9321-8 (e)

Library of Congress Control Number: 2017918439

Balboa Press rev. date: 12/05/2017

Contents

In memory of my loving wife of thirty-eight years, Susie Hoff, and her admirable battle with ovarian cancer.

To Shariann Hoff, whose remarkable love and willingness to share her life with me has made this story possible.

Acknowledgments

I would like to thank all of the friends and acquaintances who urged me to share this story.

Notably, I thank Frank and Andrea Smith, who were randomly seated next to us at an adjoining table in a restaurant. Following some discussions about our lives, they immediately and strongly advocated that I write this book as an inspiration to others.

I am also most appreciative of Sharon Whitley Larson and her husband, Carl Larson, both noted authors and journalists, for their encouragement and technical assistance in making this book a reality.

Lastly, I owe my wife, Shariann Hoff, without whom my life story would have a very different ending, the utmost gratitude for her understanding of my situation, as well as her assistance and support in creating this narrative.

Chapter 1

From the Start

Early in 2002, my wife, Susie, and I were headed to Pendaries, a small golf course in the mountains west of Las Vegas, New Mexico. We had been there several times before, and it was one of our favorites among myriad golf courses, ski resorts, and tennis facilities we had visited over the thirty-five years of our marriage. A marriage although not free of occasional turbulence, was filled with love, compromise, and an ever-growing dependence on one another's companionship.

We met in the late sixties at a party thrown by my girlfriend in a suburb of Denver. Susie was a musician. I foolishly thought I could play some banjo and sing. I was fiddling with my banjo in a bedroom when Susie entered, wondering what the strange sounds were. We talked a while, and she suggested that I acquire a better banjo. The one I had cost about twenty dollars brand-new. I thanked her for the advice, and we parted ways.

I was a national bank examiner, and a few months later, I was on assignment in Durango, Colorado. After dinner, some associates and I were looking for some entertainment. We were directed to the Full House, a bar that no longer exists, on the main street of Durango. Upon entering, we were greeted with the sounds of a folk group consisting of four young men and two young ladies. They provided their own acoustical accompaniment and were quite talented. My associates and I found ourselves gravitating there every night for the duration of our stay.

One of the two young women was Susie, and we became well acquainted during this time. I became a quasi-groupie of the Folks about Towne, and over the next several months, I made it a point to attend their performances as much as my virtually nonstop travel schedule would allow. They became a popular attraction in the Denver area.

Shortly thereafter, Susie and I chanced to both be in Durango, once again. I asked her out to lunch on our first formal date. She accepted, and thus began a relationship filled with closeness, adventure, and a somewhat nomadic existence. We were married in February 1967.

Chapter 2

Good Times

My career took us from Evergreen, a small mountain community less than an hour from Denver, to the charismatic and exciting ski resort of Aspen. Later, we went to another charming ski resort, Breckenridge. Both towns were nestled in what were at that time pristine mountains isolated from the growing urbanization of Denver. During the ski season, these towns were bustling with visitors from all corners of the world. These included actors and politicians as well as astronauts and corporate magnates from around the globe. Of note were the opportunities to meet John Wayne at an intimate New Year's Eve party, John Denver before he became famous, and Lee Marvin shortly after the release of the movie *Paint Your Wagon*. One evening, Susie and I watched John Denver play virtually all evening when we were the only folks in the audience. I was a senior officer at the only bank in town, and so we had invitations to parties where we often had opportunities to meet some of these people and visit with them in a very casual manner.

The evenings were filled with dinners at some of the finest restaurants in the state, and we enjoyed excellent live entertainment of every imaginable genre.

There was, of course, the skiing. Susie was an employee of the Aspen Skiing Corporation and was provided an unlimited family pass. We had found paradise!

What we were unprepared for was the bonus of the spring, fall, and summer months, when the out-of-town visitors cleared out of the area and the towns were left almost empty. When we moved to Breckenridge, the permanent population was fewer than seven hundred people. During the winter, it swelled to the thousands.

In Aspen, early spring brought the annual thaw. Now we could sit and watch water run down the streets. The usually crowded, noisy bank lobby was virtually silent. We could catch our breath after a winter of long days at work and too-lengthy nights of play. Thank goodness we were young!

The offseason had numerous benefits. We rode horses and took our four-wheel-drive vehicles into remote areas for overnight camping, sometimes not seeing another human for two or three days.

I was a fanatical fly fisherman and was able to fish essentially anywhere I wanted on both the Roaring Fork and the Frying Pan Rivers. I sometimes left home before dawn and did not return until after sundown, always with great success and many times without traveling more than five or ten miles from home.

We hiked through some of the most beautiful meadows, canyons, and high mountain trails imaginable, often stumbling onto ghost towns, mine tipples, and mineshafts.

Many times I fished in a stream or small lake while Susie hunted wild mushrooms. The fish and fungus, fried up in butter over a wood fire, were unforgettable.

As an accomplished musician, Susie spent a good deal of her time practicing. It paid off in Breckenridge, where she joined three young men to form a bluegrass band that enjoyed a reasonably successful season or two, considering they were all ski instructors or ski patrolmen.

The final few years in the mountain communities were spent on Missouri Heights, which was located about thirty miles downstream from Aspen, near the community of Carbondale. Here we had a small acreage and developed it into a horse setup with barn, pasture, paddocks, and a training ring. Susie had an equestrian background, and after negotiating somewhat favorably with area horse trainers and traders, she was able to hone her skills, purchase an adequate horse, and join a registered foxhunt.

In the early 1980s, our next adventure took us to the city of Grand Junction, Colorado. With much hard work and a magnificent effort, Susie became the open jumper champion of the Western Colorado Hunter Jumper Association.

When it came to music, horses, skiing, tennis, and golf, she was tenacious in study and practice until she excelled.

I supported her through the music and horsey things as a groupie, sound and light man, carpenter, horse groomer, mechanic, driver, and stall cleaner. I also treated wounds on the animals, administered vaccines, and built barns and miles of wooden fences. The materials for the fences were provided by my obtaining a US Forest Service permit to harvest trees some forty miles from our home, and by cutting those trees myself. I relieved them of their branches, hauled them back to the ranch, and built the fences—all a one-man operation. I also built irrigation systems, irrigated pastures, hauled hay, and disposed of the bounty that resulted from cleaning the stalls. All of this sounds like a great deal of work. It was, but I thoroughly enjoyed it.

Chapter 3

Changes

I was the chief executive officer of a small bank located in a suburb of Grand Junction. This took an enormous amount of my time, and so the domestic chores often lasted well into the night. The controlling ownership interest of the bank was shared equally by my brother Ron and me. Unfortunately, during a bust period in the local economy, a result of a severe downturn in petroleum prices, state and federal regulators chose to close the bank even though our capital was stronger and our loan portfolio was performing at a higher level than that of many savings and loans associations that remained open. I learned to be extremely wary of government bureaucracies. Our hard-earned assets and hopes for a secure future vanished overnight.

Shortly thereafter, Ron asked if I would be interested in joining him in marketing his large landscaping business in the Denver area. After the whipping we had received at the hands of regulators, Susie and I accepted the offer. A career that had provided us with an amazing life while we realized the satisfaction of helping individuals build their lives and supporting these small communities' growth now seemed to be at an end, and all for some political motive that I have yet to thoroughly understand.

We moved to Parker, Colorado, and for the next three years enjoyed the lack of pressure from my former vocation. We were close to my family—something I had not experienced for over fifteen years. Susie had access to excellent training personnel in dressage, an equestrian format that requires a gifted horse and a highly experienced rider with extraordinary patience. Before leaving the Grand Junction area, she had purchased a magnificent Trakehner, a warmblood breed that excels in this discipline. Although we both worked very hard to make ends meet, this was a period in our lives together that was somewhat free of the horrible pressures of the last several months of the failed bank.

At this point, I must extend my heartfelt appreciation to Ron and his wife, Sheila, for their understanding and generosity in helping us move forward from a traumatic experience to rebuilding our lives. Many families become severely divided over financial losses such as this. Rather than spurn us, my brother and sister-in-law extended a warm and helpful hand for which I have never thanked them enough.

I worked with Ron for about two years, during which I learned more about landscaping design, sales, and snow plowing than I had ever imagined I could. We got along rather well, considering I had been a CEO of three different banks at this point and was now being supervised by my younger brother. It takes a real trauma in some lives to teach humility.

Around the end of this two-year period, our needs for cash flow exceeded what the landscape company could support, and I chanced to meet Scott, the CEO of a small real estate mortgage company located in the Denver area. Scott and his partner were seeking someone to contact commercial banks in the state and persuade them to establish a relationship whereby the banks would funnel home mortgages, which many smaller banks were not prepared to retain in their own portfolios, to the mortgage company. We worked out an agreement, and through this relationship, Scott and I became close friends. The mortgage market collapsed soon thereafter, Scott's company closed down, and the two of us worked closely together to find an alternate means to support our families. Many opportunities surfaced, and a few met with limited success. It was enough to get us both by for the next few months.

A momentous event occurred for both of us when Scott accepted an offer to assist a large mortgage company in Houston, Texas, begin its recovery from the devastating effects of the recent downturn. He had commuted from Denver to Houston weekly for about a month when I received a call from him asking if I had an interest in contracting with the company for a period of one month to assist in managing the recovery process. The offer seemed lucrative considering my other nonexistent options. I agreed, and the following Sunday I embarked on a life-changing adventure. The one-month contract became a thirteen-month whirlwind of commuting between Denver and Houston. Susie and I alternated weekends, with her flying to Houston followed by my flying to Denver, and then my remaining in Houston and Susie in Denver on the third weekend. This schedule was repeated for many months.

Toward the end of this thirteen-month period, the East Coast bank that owned the mortgage company offered me a full-time position, which I accepted. My supervising officer was offered a position at a sizeable mortgage company in Austin, Texas, which he accepted. Scott had already returned to a position in Denver to be with his family.

Within a month, my former supervisor, now in Austin, called and asked if I would be interested in interviewing for a vice president's position with his new company. I did. The interview resulted in an offer, and I accepted. Susie and I moved from Parker to Austin a short time later.

Just over a year earlier, I could barely spell mortgage, and now I was an officer in a respected Texas company. Wow! None of this was in my plan just a few short years ago.

The company grew, was merged with another company, and through it all, I progressed financially and was made a senior vice president. The salary became very comfortable, and the bonuses even more so. Susie and I bought a small house on a golf course, and she learned the game. It was as secure as we had felt in many years. We now spent more time together, playing golf; working with her one remaining horse; doting on our white standard poodle, Boomer; traveling; and enjoying Austin. It was a good time for us—but nothing lasts forever.

Our next adventure began with a phone call from a former associate and friend, with whom I had examined banks out of Denver. He had left the examining career and had become employed by a bank in the small community of Canon City, Colorado. Over the years, he had obtained stock in the bank a little at a time, and now owned controlling interest in a holding company that owned the primary bank as well as four other community banks. The president and CEO of one of the affiliated banks in Pueblo, Colorado, was retiring, and my friend offered that position to me.

When Susie and I first moved to Texas, she had resisted rather strongly. She was now enjoying it immensely. When we discussed the offer to return to Colorado, we made a joint decision to decline because we were quite happy with our present situation. For my friend, that was not an adequate explanation, and he virtually pleaded with me to fly back with Susie to discuss the offer, so we did.

With my friend, we toured the bank, explored the residential areas, visited the country club, and had a dinner attended by senior officers of the banks, along with their spouses. It was quite a sales pitch, and certainly for me, it was alluring compared to the now bureaucratic structure of my present employer. My friend insisted that I meet him for breakfast the following morning to discuss some of the details that he had in mind, as well as to answer any questions that I had concerning the bank. We met, and although I had some important things to discuss with Susie, I leaned heavily toward the move.

For the balance of that day, we embarked on a discovery tour on our own, during which Susie expressed her concerns with living in the rather arid climate of Pueblo. It was winter, and everything in the area was brown and dull. It was much greener in central Texas.

We flew back to Austin the following day. Once settled back at home, I discussed several of the points my friend had to offer at our private meeting. The first was compensation. Although the salary was less than I was currently earning, I had negotiated a rather lucrative bonus plan that was based on performance. The second was the holding companies' employee stock ownership plan (ESOP). The plan was based on holding company performance, and all contributions were from the company. The plan had a fine record, and there was no indication that anything less could be expected. The third was stock options. I had a minor program with the present employer. My friend offered a reasonable option plan, but because I was fifty-three years old and was making my umpteenth career move, I requested that he double the option to enhance retirement security. Surprisingly he agreed, however a portion was from his personal portfolio.

The fourth point that he had made regarded my job security. My friend was well aware that companies such as my current employer were notorious for being restructured through sales or acquisitions. I was in upper middle management and was vulnerable to any such change, however insignificant. He offered me job security.

Susie and I discussed the issue thoroughly, with my lobbying heavily in favor of the move. The issues of job security and stock options were enough to finally convince her that the move was best for our financial future.

We returned to Pueblo shortly thereafter to search for a home, and as luck would have it, one of the bank's vendors from Canon City owned a home on the golf course in Pueblo West, a development about five miles west of Pueblo. He was preparing to put it on the market. We secured the home, returned to Texas, and began preparations for our move back to colorful Colorado!

With most moves to a top management position, there are many issues that arise, and they tend to derail the plans and projections of the new arrival. This was no exception. There were operational issues, human resource issues, regulatory issues, fixed asset issues, and of course "new guy" nerve issues. I found myself buried in the quagmire for a full year, working long hours and weeks and feeling very alone in my mission.

Meanwhile, Susie was being introduced to the ladies' golf leagues at the country club, and she was rapidly developing close friendships. She became a different person than I had known in Austin. Where before she was rather reclusive when I was not around, she began inviting couples to our home for dinners and parties. Many were business owners in the area and became customers of the bank. She was carrying out the personal call, marketing programs that I had no time to perform. She was bringing them home to me, and we had not even discussed it. In addition, we became friends with many of these couples and would enjoy these relationships for many years to come.

Chapter 4

Unexpected Loss

About two years into our Pueblo experience, I received an alarming call from one of my siblings. My mother had suffered some type of seizure while relaxing with my sister, Kathy, on the beach at Lake McConaughy, Nebraska.

Mother had lived in Denver, and more recently she had returned to Alliance, Nebraska, to be nearer Kathy and my brother Gordon, both of who lived in the area, and with whom she had been somewhat physically estranged for many years due to the distance from Denver. She also found there a retirement complex that was more affordable and allowed her more independence than she had experienced at her previous quarters in Denver.

Susie and I followed the sequence of events that took my mother to a small rural hospital and then by ambulance to a hospital with a neurology center in Kearney, Nebraska. Once she was situated in the ICU there, my brother Ron arranged for a charter plane to gather himself, my sister Carolyn, and my brother Sam at Centennial Airport, near Denver. pick me up at Pueblo Memorial Airport and then proceed to Kearney.

The Beechcraft King Air handled the flight well, had a great pilot, and provided beer and snacks. My brothers had some beer, but fearing an explosive bladder, I declined. We landed in Kearney, where the person manning the fixed-base facility graciously offered his personal vehicle as our transportation to the hospital. We had made arrangements for the pilot to hold the plane there for the duration of our short visit.

We arrived at the hospital to find our two Nebraska siblings waiting in the ICU area. Mother was unconscious, and it appeared highly unlikely that she would regain consciousness because she had suffered a ruptured blood vessel in the brain. The best presumption that the neurologists could make was that the escaped fluid had damaged a significant number of brain cells, and the situation was quite likely irreversible. We took turns individually visiting her bedside at hourly intervals, as allowed by hospital protocol. When we had each let her know we were there in our various ways, those of us from Colorado were compelled to return to the airport and make the return trip.

Our younger sister Kathy would remain with mother. Within days, it was determined that although the prognosis was not good, the Kearney hospital did not have the level of equipment or expertise that was available at a suburban Denver hospital to make a final determination. The family voted unanimously to fly our mother back to Denver via air ambulance for further tests. We each had a role to play because arrangements had to be made at both hospitals for the transfer, and the air ambulance had to be procured. It was my responsibility to secure the appropriate plane for her transfer, and I had a friend and customer who was in the business. All arrangements were made, and within a few days from our trip to Kearney, she was safely transported to the Denver-area hospital.

Mother remained under close observation for some period. She would occasionally regain consciousness, but any communication was of things that occurred long past, or she was completely unintelligible. She would lose consciousness soon after any such incident. One day, as my two sisters and I were walking in the hallway with the lead neurologist, we asked her for her advice on continuing hospitalization. Her prognosis was that the situation was totally irreversible, and that our mother would remain in the current state permanently. Her best advice was to place mother in a hospice and allow her to pass comfortably without the life support she was now on. Tears flowed freely from all of us, including the neurologist, as we discussed this very difficult decision. We gave her our permission, and she made the necessary arrangements.

Within ten days, my mother was gone. She had to suffer the death of her husband and our father forty years before, and she had devoted her entire life to making certain that her children were loved and guided to fulfilled lives. She'd raised six children who ranged in age from five to eighteen years old when she'd become a widow and single mother. She never had interest in another man, and she worked tirelessly to see that we were raised knowing appropriate manners, speaking proper English, and treating others as we would want to be treated ourselves. She was a resounding success, and through it all we each returned her love generously in our own distinctive ways.

It has been twenty years since her passing, and I continue to miss her immeasurably.

Chapter 5

Back on Track

I woke one morning to find that the bank was now in the good graces of the regulators, there was growth in the loan portfolio, and earnings were improving. The one thing that had slipped through during the time that my head was buried in regulatory and operating reports was staffing. Most people who'd been employed prior to my arrival had been there for many years, and they were well meaning. The dilemma was lack of training, redundancy in duties, and morale. The result was an inefficient operation, providing an unacceptable level of customer service. I attempted to utilize all personnel in a new structure and provide appropriate training. Unfortunately, for many people, change is problematic. It took about three additional years before we managed to assemble a staff of well-trained personnel who took pride in their positions and in their bank. Once the staffing issues were resolved, I had more time to become involved in the community.

In previous locations, I had overwhelmed myself by spending an inordinate number of hours serving the communities. I was president of professional organizations, chambers of commerce, and resort associations. I even served on a town council at one time. Not this time around. I chose just one organization, the local 4-H foundation, and devoted all community service time to enhancing educational opportunities for the 4-H members in our community by raising funds for scholarships. This decision provided much more time for Susie and me to be together.

Now four years into this venture, things were going smoothly for us. We enjoyed playing golf with our newfound friends, and we were able to travel extensively. Frequently, we visited friends on both coasts. We were close to the mountains that we loved, and we enjoyed each other's company probably more than ever before. We once again had financial security.

For an additional four years, we enjoyed the fruits of our early endeavors. The banks grew, the holding company grew, and we once again could look to our future. We upgraded our home, purchased an automobile that was more than just functional, dined out more often, and traveled whenever the opportunity presented itself. On virtually every occasion that an acquaintance mentioned a golf course or resort that we had not yet played, within a few months we had conquered that barrier.

Had it not been for my boss friend's battle with a bipolar disorder that could cause extensive stress from time to time, these four years would have been the essence of a textbook relationship between two people after thirty-five years of marriage.

Chapter 6

Frightening News

This brings me back to Pendaries, the golf course in New Mexico. The course is nestled among the ponderosa pines at about eight thousand feet, and it overlooks the Sangre de Cristo Mountains and the Rociada Valley. Susie and I stayed in the resort's comfortable guest rooms.

On the final day of our stay, we were approaching an elevated tee, the access to which required about ten steps up a rather steep incline. I noticed Susie seemed to be struggling for breath as we neared the top. I asked if she was all right, and she responded that she thought she was almost not going to make it. We completed that hole, and as her labored breathing continued, we decided to quit. At this point, she thought that it might be best if we visited the nearest emergency room. I agreed.

We retreated toward Taos, the nearest community harboring a hospital. As we neared the town, she felt that she was improving. It occurred to both of us that it might have been the change in elevation that had caused the problem. By the time we reached Taos, she felt significantly better, and so we decided to continue home. We did, and that evening she once again felt normal.

Over the next several days, Susie experienced flare-ups of the breathing issue as well as extraordinary heartburn. She visited our family internist, who put her with a physician's assistant. This person prescribed antacids and nothing more. The visits to the doctor's office were made almost daily for about a week.

Then one night when I was sleeping soundly, I was awakened by moans and shrieks of pain from Susie that sent a high level of fear and chills through my body. We dressed quickly and proceeded to the emergency room, where she was treated with anything but compassion. It took forever for a triage nurse to examine her, and after a wait of hours, we entered the treatment area. She waited hours more while the staff was enjoying lengthy discussions of their private lives along with a lot of good laughs. My pleading for them to ease her pain was met with shrugs and scowls.

Finally she was examined, and it was determined that she had an extensive buildup of fluid in her abdominal cavity. The next morning the fluid was extracted, which gave her much-needed relief. After further analysis of the fluids, our soon-to-be-terminated internist called to let us know that tumorous cells had been discovered in the fluid, but he said nothing more. He apparently did not have the courage to face Susie and me to explain what was happening.

A close friend of ours, who was also an internist, stopped by to visit, and I will never forget Susie's words. "Barry, will you be my doctor?"

His reply was, "Of course."

With that change, information flowed, and we were faced with her diagnosis of stage four ovarian cancer. I had never been so void of words or solutions in my life. Although he possessed a very buoyant attitude, the oncologist had no choice but to give her an estimate of three to five years. Our lives had changed overnight, and what followed was miraculous, tragic, heartwarming, and very sad.

Almost immediately, Susie faced major surgery to remove the organs that harbored the killer cells. Following this traumatic procedure, she was left a weak and seemingly vanquished remnant of her former self. In spite of all medical personnel urging her to ingest calories in any form for her to survive, she had no interest in eating anything. Finally, a feeding tube was inserted into her abdominal area, and a pump was attached to provide her with some nutrition.

It was fortunate that I now had a highly competent staff to support us at the bank. With the exception of an hour to retreat to our home to shave and shower and an occasional trip to the bank to check on things or attend a meeting, I was now spending twenty-four hours a day at her bedside. My sleep came in the form of a few hours tossing around on a welcome, but less than comfortable, recliner chair that the exceptionally supportive medical staff probably hocked their souls to obtain. Once in a while, a friend would drop by and visit with her so that I could retreat to a local restaurant and suppress my hidden, but very tangible, discouragement and disheartenment through a large, stiff martini and a meal. This would allow me to return to the hospital and resume my role as an upbeat and positive influence.

No matter what form of diversion I attempted, my mind could not escape the fear and hopelessness that I felt. I found myself sitting at traffic lights on the way home to shower, sobbing uncontrollably. I would look up and find that people in nearby vehicles were staring at me. Most often this would occur without my realizing that it was happening, until a horn behind urged me to proceed.

A couple of weeks passed, and although Susie was progressing in the physical healing of the surgical area, she was not improving in the mental sense. She seemed to have regressed in her desire to live. When urged by the medical staff to walk as much as possible, she would cooperate. I would walk with her, wheeling the intravenous tower with its many bags and tubes, up and down these now stark hallways. However, she never showed improvement in her energy and appetite levels. We were both warned that if she did not begin a more normal diet, it could affect her digestive process and significantly reduce her chance of survival. Our family doctor later informed me that he did not expect her to leave the hospital alive.

She did leave, and she was transferred to the skilled nursing unit of the hospital that provided less intense care but also had a more cheerful ambience. Susie finally agreed to eat custard, which had to have very specific ratios of egg, sugar, and vanilla to be accepted by her. I was now baking custard in rather large quantities on my trips home to shave and shower. This was an encouraging breakthrough for me.

One of the nurses in this unit was particularly helpful in mentoring Susie not just in the medical sense but also in life issues. She dwelt on the positive things in survival. Previously, the medical staff had consistently presented the treatment options as "You must perform this function, or you chances of survival are diminished." This new and more successful approach was, "If you perform this function, your survival opportunities are enhanced—and look at all you can do once you have recovered!" I believe that this input was a turning point that would ultimately make the difference between Susie possibly losing her battle over the next few months, or recovering and living for the next three years in a fulfilling manner.

We spent a total of four weeks in this unit. I continued to sleep on the recliner, and although Susie was not making major strides, she was more cooperative. She even occasionally volunteered to walk the hallways. I continued to follow her with the tower, but with fewer bags and tubes.

It was finally time to take her home. The preparation included having a home health care supply house deliver all of the things we were presently accustomed to in the hospital: a hospital bed, an intravenous tower, an oxygen cart and tanks, a wheelchair, a supply of the nutrient goop that was being pumped into her stomach, and of course the pump with which to supply it to her. I envisioned a cheerful, helpful person coming to the house and assisting me in setting up all of this equipment in anticipation of Susie's arrival. What I got was a bunch of well-worn equipment dumped in the house and left for me to assemble and learn to operate.

I moved the king-sized bed to one side of the room and leaned both the frame and mattress set against the wall. This allowed room for the hospital bed, the tower, a wheeled bedside table, accessibility for nurses and physical therapists, and our own plush recliner chair for my sleeping comfort. Fortunately, I was able to comprehend the intricacies of the adjustable bed and had it functional in less than six hours. The rest was relatively easy.

I picked Susie up at the hospital. She was extremely weak, but I soon had her home with the help of the wheelchair from auto to door. The nurses had given me a course on the feeding pump and the oxygen supply before we left the hospital. Soon I had her in bed, and all of the machines seemed to be functioning properly. She fell asleep, and I was able to retreat to the kitchen and prepare my own martini. Things had improved for both of us.

Although I felt alone and somewhat helpless, I was soon to be surprised by the competency of the home nurses provided by the agency. The most supportive thing that occurred was a ring of the doorbell. Upon my opening the door, I faced Barry, our doctor and, more important, magnificent friend. He was there to ascertain her well-being. He would visit her regularly for the next few weeks without any requests from us. This was another major influence in her progress.

The skilled nursing group at the hospital had scheduled the first appointment for chemotherapy, and with the aid of the wheelchair, we proceeded to the oncologist at the cancer treatment facility. I wheeled Susie into the waiting room of the oncologist's office, and after a reasonable wait, we were ushered in by a very upbeat and encouraging nurse. Over the next few years, we found that the staff in this facility were devoted, compassionate, and extremely professional.

After a short wait in the examining room, the doctor entered and took one look at Susie. He was dumbfounded that she was too weak to visit his office without a wheelchair. He announced that her CA-125 reading, a marker used to possibly detect, confirm, or monitor ovarian cancer, was at a very high level, in the thousands. She needed to begin chemotherapy immediately. Unfortunately, the doctor found her too weak to tolerate the treatment, and he sent her home for two weeks before he would consider it again.

During this waiting period, I had a call from the woman who owned the stables where Susie's only remaining horse, Derby, was kept. The aging horse was suffering from an acute case of colic. The vet was there and had determined that it was untreatable. She was calling for permission to have Susie's prize gelding euthanized!

In her weakened condition and in her pajamas, Susie had me help her to the car and drive her to the stable. The horse was lying on its side and taking labored, shallow breaths. Susie leapt from the car, climbed the fence, and dropped to the other side. She knelt by the dying animal, petted him gently, and spoke softly into his ear. She climbed back over the fence, gave the vet permission, and returned to the car. She directed me to return home and sobbed the entire way back. She would break into tears each time we passed by the stable for the rest of her life.

The doctor's refusing to administer chemotherapy was the event that would inspire Susie to live her remaining time to its fullest. She could barely walk to the bathroom when she arrived home from the hospital, and she seldom left the bed. Now, having realized that she was in grave danger in the short term, she began a valiant battle. To regain her strength, she walked to the end of the hallway dozens of times, then to the far end of the house scores of times, and finally to the end of the driveway, down the street, and then a mile or more. All of that occurred within the two-week period. At first, I followed her with oxygen, then for a while she carried it herself, and then she required none at all.

Chapter 7

Hope

Susie returned to a very pleased oncologist, and she readily tolerated her chemotherapy, in part due to the valiant efforts of the nurses and other technicians in the treatment facility to make the process as comfortable as possible and successfully lift the spirits of the patients. She lost her aversion to food and was now eating whatever was necessary to regain her strength. Soon the feeding tube was removed—a glorious day for me—and we were faced with only small oxygen bottles between her and total independence. She was losing her hair as a side effect of the chemotherapy, but we shopped locally and on the internet for acceptable wigs. Soon that hurdle was behind us.

During her recovery, we received a call from a woman in Taos, New Mexico, regarding standard poodle pups that the woman had bred, and that would soon be available. We were aware of her through close Aspen friends who had moved to Santa Fe, a short distance from Taos, and had purchased a pup from her. We'd had a remarkable standard poodle, Boomer, before, and had lost him to old age a year or so ago. I suggested that as a diversion from our now rather mundane routine, we take an overnight trip to Taos to look at the pups. Susie agreed, and with the doctor's blessing, we departed.

We had an enjoyable drive to Taos and checked into a comfortable hotel. Susie was now able to go extended periods without the oxygen, which allowed us to go out to dinner without the tanks. I did place one in the car just in case, however it was unnecessary. This dinner, although not gourmet, was a definite milestone in her recovery, and it was the most pleasant evening we had spent in the two months since her initial diagnosis.

The next morning, we made an appointment to meet the puppies. Following our morning rituals, we proceeded to the home of the poodle breeder for our first meeting. As I recall, there were thirteen puppies in all, and because no one had yet committed, we had our pick. We "interviewed" them all—several times, actually. Only one was severely distracted by our presence, and it returned to jump into our laps and generously kiss us both the entire time we were there. It was, of course, the runt of the litter.

We returned home and, after about eighteen hours of discussion, decided we must return and make a choice before we lost both of our favorites. It was only about a three hour-drive, and so we drove back to Taos on a day trip and gave the runt and another one our full attention. There was never any doubt. We were the littlest poodle's choice. He saw us before we got close to the kennel and nearly broke the door down to get to us. This little black guy was a world-class salesman. Susie was happier and smiling more than I had seen in years. We purchased him immediately and left, leaving him there because the owner felt that he needed a couple of more weeks with his mother and siblings before being weaned.

During the waiting period, we discovered a Chevrolet minivan that would allow a dog in the rear area access to the front seats through the space between the seats, where a console normally was located. Previous dogs invariably leaped over the backs of the driver and passenger seats to get to the front when they were left alone for a few minutes. We traded our relatively new Chevy Impala for one of these vans, with all of the accessories one could imagine. It proved to be an excellent decision given our circumstances.

Armed with our new vehicle, we set off to pick up the new addition to our family. We had previously ranked possible names for this little critter, and although I had many thoughts other than Cowboy, Susie was unrelenting in her top choice. The name stuck. We picked him up and left his birthplace. He stood in Susie's lap with his large, puppy paws on the passenger door window, and he looked back toward the kennel as we departed. He kept his eyes turned toward it for about a minute and gave a rather quiet puppy whimper. Then he turned his face toward Susie, licked her on the cheek, and promptly moved to the floor behind her seat and went to sleep. He never whimpered again. He had never been in an automobile before and had only one tiny, almost undetectable accident during the trip home. He would beg to go with us when we left in the automobile from that point forward.

Cowboy was the best therapeutic thing that could have happened. His companionship quickly softened the blow of Derby's death, as well as diverted Susie's concerns from her own dire situation to his well-being and training. It was an amazing turnaround in a short period of time.

The chemo continued, and we had to endure the loss of her hair. I recall the first time while assisting washing her hair. I applied the shampoo, and with the first attempt to work it in, a clump of hair was left in my hand. She apparently had mentally prepared herself for this, and other than a disgusted acknowledgment, she moved forward without complaint. Soon she was bald. We searched throughout the city for acceptable wigs, but none worked well for her. I began an online search and soon located some that appeared to be what she wanted. We ordered several, kept a few, and returned the rest. Before long, she was comfortable with occasionally plopping on her wig and going out in the community.

We now began stepping onto the fairway of the golf course, which our back patio faced. Here, I assisted Susie in regaining her balance and her once textbook golf swing. Susie made remarkable progress. Soon she stood on the number one tee at the country club, and a group of her closest golfing pals and their husbands surrounded the tee and applauded loudly when she hit her drive down the middle of the fairway—the first since that awful ovarian cancer awakening almost three months before.

After many weeks of chemotherapy, Susie entered the oncologist's office following the customary blood tests. Her CA-125 marker was at a count in the low double digits. He announced that she was currently free of the cancer and would no longer require chemo. We were elated! All ports were removed, and we returned to a normal life.

Thus began the saga of the Irish Tenors.

Chapter 8

The Groupie

Susie had seen the Irish group on public television and had purchased one or two of their CDs. She was entranced with their music, and the first time they appeared nearby (I believe in Denver), we were off to see them.

Although Susie had the ultimate regard for all three of the tenors (Finbar Wright, Anthony Kearns, and Ronan Tynan), she immediately became infatuated with her favorite, Anthony Kearns. She could not resist his boyish looks and golden voice. Little was I prepared for this new journey.

The trio's tours were worldwide. Susie had no interest in traveling abroad with the uncertainty of her health in the back of her mind, but their appearances in the United States were extensive, and I would search for any within the lower forty-eight states, to which we might have access.

For the next two and a half years, we had three things to which every now-cherished moment would be devoted: Cowboy, the Irish Tenors, and golf, probably in that order.

The weeks brought growth but little maturity to Cowboy. He displayed nonstop energy but also an equal amount of love for Susie. When he was considered old enough, Susie enrolled the two of them in an obedience class, which was held at the Colorado State Fairgrounds in Pueblo. He proved to be extremely intelligent and willing to please. His rapid progress was a thrill to us both and fortified the bond between the two of them. I don't believe there was anything in the world that could have created more joy for Susie during her final months.

The icing on this happening was that she discovered a kennel and grooming facility nearby that employed a young woman who earned Susie's complete trust, as well as Cowboy's complete respect and adoration. It has been so long since all of this transpired that I have forgotten her name, but should she ever read this script, I hope she will contact me so that I might thank her.

We could take this lovely animal to her for either boarding or grooming, and not only would he go willingly, but he'd actually get so excited about seeing this new addition to his family that he often forgot to say goodbye to us when we left him with her. This made leaving him for travel a cinch. We believed that he looked forward to our trips more than we did!

This brings me to the next item on the list of diversions from Susie's condition: The Irish Tenors. Susie was so smitten with Anthony Kearns that she became the ultimate groupie! We would divert our world to see him at every opportunity, and when we did arrive at a concert, she took advantage of any occasion where she might make direct contact with him, including meet-and-greet affairs that sometimes lasted until after midnight. Many times we had early flights to catch the next day, but the energy from her excitement carried her through.

At one point in Cleveland, we chanced upon Anthony in the elevator of his hotel. Notice, *his* hotel, not ours. Susie approached him with me by her side, and she told him of her great admiration for him and his talent. She then noticed me standing there and promptly said, "And I would like you to meet my husband, Harvey."

With like promptness, he stated, "Good to meet you. How you keepin'?"

He had no idea who she was, but he was now on a first name basis with her husband.

The next time she had an opportunity to speak to him, she related that story to him, including how cute she thought "How you keepin'?" was. From that point forward, whenever he spotted her, he would greet her with, "How you keepin'?"

For as many months as she was able, we followed the trio to many venues, including Santa Fe, New Mexico; Boise, Idaho; Cleveland, Ohio; Milwaukee, Wisconsin; Naples, Florida; Cape Cod, Massachusetts (Twice.); San Marcos, California; Colorado Springs, Colorado; Denver, Colorado; and I am sure several more that I have forgotten.

I must thank these talented people for the pleasure they brought to Susie during this difficult time.

Chapter 9

Once in a Lifetime

Susie had adapted well to the Pueblo version of country club life. Although some members came from wealthy backgrounds, most were self-made business leaders in the community. Although they were slightly cliquish, they were also friendly, welcoming, and supportive of new members of both the club and the community. She began playing golf on a regular basis with her newfound friends, and she quickly ranked among the better players. Her stature with them was elevated when she was asked to represent women golfers on the club's golf committee. She was instrumental in having a rule rescinded that restricted female players from beginning play on the weekends before 11:00 a.m.

We played together often, and we entered and won the club couples' championship one year. Whenever we planned a trip away from home, we planned it around golf courses at the destination, as well as along the way if it were a road trip. This practice allowed us to play some famous courses, such as the TPC at Sawgrass, where Susie shot an excellent round that included a birdie on a three par—while I proceeded to bungle every hole on the course.

We continued this travel routine following her remission from the cancer. During this period, we played Cranberry Valley Golf Club on Cape Cod, Brown Deer Park in Milwaukee, and many other courses across the country. We travelled with friends to Santa Fe, New Mexico, where Susie logged her one and only hole-in-one on a three par at the Black Mesa Golf Course. I believe this was on the same trip we took to visit the Irish Tenors in Santa Fe. If it had not come on its own, I would have paid all that I owned to have that hole-in-one occur for her, so that I could experience her joy and excitement of that day.

Chapter 10

My Turn

In June 2003, we were once again on our way to Pendaries, near Las Vegas, New Mexico. It was a trip to complete the round of golf that we had left a year and a half before to tend to the symptoms that were the result of Susie's cancer.

We stopped at a gas station in Las Vegas to refuel and get a bite to eat in the little Mexican deli inside. Susie picked a taco or burrito. I was not too ravenous and chose some chicharrones, or fried pork rinds. We then proceeded to the golf resort, about an hour's drive away. When we arrived, there was an ominous cloud overhead. We were just exiting the car when it began to rain, hail, and blow horrendously. A bolt of lightning struck and immediately thundered with an explosive force that shook the car and our nerves. We jumped back into the vehicle, and I quickly parked under a very large pine tree, where we waited out the meteorological onslaught. At the end, there were branches, leaves, and building parts strewn wherever we gazed.

We entered the clubhouse to inquire about the status of our afternoon tee time. Not unexpectedly, we were informed that it was canceled until the next morning due to the two to three inches of hail remaining on the course.

We were planning to spend a couple of nights and so decided to return to Las Vegas for dinner. We received recommendations from the people at the golf club and proceeded to check them out. Fortunately, the town is home to New Mexico Highlands University, has a population of about fourteen thousand, and features a couple of very nice restaurants. We chose one, entered, were seated, and ordered a drink while we reviewed the menu.

Just after the drinks arrived, I began feeling a little nauseous. I excused myself to the men's room. Nothing really happened there, so I decided to walk around a little outside. I couldn't shake that feeling, and I told Susie to go ahead and order while I sat in the car for a few minutes. I sat in the driver's seat, reclined it back as far as it would go, and closed my eyes. The next thing I knew, Susie and another person were standing over me with the car door opened. I was covered in vomit but didn't remember it happening. I felt another surge coming on, but the same thing occurred. I blacked out both times just before I heaved.

The people who had stopped offered to lead us to the emergency room at the local hospital. Once there, I sat in the waiting area for only a couple of minutes because it was obvious if someone didn't do something fairly quickly, they were going to be dealing with a sizeable bit of untidiness!

I was on the examining table with a doctor and a couple of assistants hovering over me. Susie was standing nearby, and the two of us were trying to explain what had happened when I apparently felt that a demonstration would be more appropriate. No further explanation was necessary. I did my deed while passing out and came to when I was all through.

I then remembered the snack purchased at the gas station, and I suggested food poisoning. Blood tests were taken, and it was confirmed. A quick hypo, and the nausea and vomiting were over. Because of my passing out, the doctor held me overnight for observation.

We asked about accommodations for Susie, and she was offered a bed in a room in the hospital, not too far from mine.

The next morning, I awoke feeling fine, but Susie was not feeling well. Her room turned out to be very cold, and there were insufficient blankets to warm her. She felt as if she had a serious cold or respiratory ailment of some nature. We were very careful to avoid such issues because her ability to resist this type of intrusion was unknown. We asked if she could be seen by a resident physician, and she was referred to the emergency room. There, she was treated very poorly by a physician I had noticed the previous night. He was unshaven, his hair was in dreadlocks that had apparently not been washed for a very long time, and he was very poorly dressed. This person was so insolent and crude that Susie came into my room crying. Fortunately, he had prescribed the correct medication, and she began feeling better.

I was getting ready to shower in preparation to be released when the doctor entered the room and announced that he was transferring me to the ICU. I was subjected to a battery of questions regarding my having felt faint or passing out prior to this incident. I had not. I was then informed that I had been monitored overnight, and my heartbeat was frequently pausing for five to eight seconds. The medical staff was amazed that I had not been passing out, or at least feeling a major sensation, when these pauses occurred. I was transferred to ICU, and we arranged a motel room for Susie.

The doctor who was treating me contacted my personal physician, Barry, as well as my cardiologist. They agreed that I should be monitored for a period of forty-eight hours and undergo tests that were customary for these symptoms. I was stuck in the hospital for at least two more nights.

I am not accustomed to sitting or lying around all day, and the confinement scheduled for me over the next two days was unbearable. I begged the ICU nurses to allow me to walk the hallways to get exercise. They responded by locating a remote monitor and acquiring the doctor's permission allowing me to roam at will. I did so, and without fail while I was out exploring this tiny hospital's hallways, a nurse would come rushing to me, out of breath and hollering, "Harvey, are you all right?"

I always responded, "Of course." They would then ask if I had felt any sensation, which I had not. I was always informed that my heart had stopped for seven to nine seconds. This chain of events occurred numerable times during my stay.

The monitoring period ended, and the doctors conferred to determine the next course of action. The announcement of that course of action stunned me. They planned on installing the dreaded old man's device, the pacemaker! I think my heart stopped for more than a few seconds upon hearing that.

I was about sixty miles from Santa Fe, the nearest large city with a hospital equipped to deal with my procedure, and I was about 215 miles from Pueblo and home. After consultations with my cardiologist in Pueblo and a cardiologist in Santa Fe, the health insurance company decided that because it was necessary to transport me by ambulance, the most economical approach was to conduct the procedure in Santa Fe. Everyone but Susie and I agreed. They ordered an ambulance to take me to Santa Fe.

The ambulance ride was uneventful, and I soon found myself in a semiprivate room because the facility was rather crowded.

Unfortunately, the person with whom I shared the room was a poor bloke who had been in an automobile accident, and he was so broken up that he had been fitted with a compression suit. I had no problem with the compression suit, however his condition required that the pressure in the suit be varied periodically. As I tried to sleep, the compressor alternated between on and off, to the point where I lay there waiting for its next move. The patient was a young Hispanic man, and in addition to the compressor, his young wife and one or two children stayed with him night and day, sleeping on the floor. There were occasional slumber interruptions with some of those things that kids do. I occasionally pitied myself a little, but my heart went out to this poor young family for their dilemma.

When the cardiologist came by to discuss the procedure, in addition to explaining how they insert wires through blood vessels into one's heart, she also explained the many things that were off-limits following the surgery. The most important to me was driving. I could not drive for two or three weeks. After discussing our returning home, the biggest concern was Susie being alone with me for a four- or five-hour drive in the event that I experienced a problem. She was a great driver but seldom drove on the longer trips. We called our friends Stan and Cindy Herman, who gladly jumped in their SUV and came running to our aid.

For all of the hoopla that preceded it, the procedure was rather simple. I recall waking before the procedure was complete, after the anesthesia had expired. The cardiologist said she would attempt to finish if I wanted, and of course if the pain was too great, she would stop and administer something to alleviate it. She attached the wire leads now running from my heart, stretched the incision, and shoved the device into place. Stretching the incision caused a bit of squealing on my part, but it took only a few seconds and was better than taking the time for a local anesthetic to become effective.

Susie had been staying in a nearby hotel, where Stan and Cindy joined her upon their arrival. They went out to lunch, and Susie noticed a black poodle being trained as a service animal. She approached the lady doing the training and, after some conversation, discovered that the dog was a brother to Cowboy! Upon my returning to my room, Cowboy's brother was there with his trainer, Susie; Stan and Cindy; and the nurses who had arranged for the visit by the service dog for therapeutic purposes. It was just that. I had been so concerned with my own situation that I had blocked out how insignificant it was overall, particularly in light of Susie's troubles.

I spent one more sleepless night, and then it was finally time to head home. That morning, Susie and I swore that we would never step foot on Pendaries soil again. The cardiologist gave us final instructions, and we began the trek homeward. Susie drove our vehicle with Cindy riding shotgun, and I rode with Stan in the SUV. When we arrived at Raton, New Mexico, just south of the Colorado border, we stopped at a Sizzler Steakhouse for lunch. I hadn't been to one for years, but I tell you, it was like a gourmet feast to me. It was the first decent food that had been served to me since the food poisoning had struck about a week before. The hospitals had kept me on their version of a heart-healthy diet!

We arrived home without incident, and for several days I was required to keep my left arm held at a specific angle, supported by a very uncomfortable sling. I had to be chauffeured everywhere I went for a couple of weeks, and I was not allowed to play any golf for two months. My home cardiologist did give me a little break of about two weeks on that last one.

Susie carted me to and from work, and the transition was smooth. Through the entire ordeal, Susie treated me as if she had no problems and as though I were the one dealing with terminal illness.

Chapter 11

Double Despair

Several months later, we visited Susie's oncologist for a routine checkup. The blood tests revealed an extraordinarily high level of the CA-125 marker. This was not good news. Both of our hearts dropped with a resounding thud. The prognosis was that she probably had a year, possibly more, to live. She had to begin taking strong doses of chemo once again. She proceeded with the treatments once more, displaying a positive and pleasant attitude. Her hair had grown back, but it was again time for the wigs.

This time we felt it necessary to get a second opinion to ascertain that the course of action was the most appropriate. We reviewed many options, and she chose the MD Anderson Cancer Center in Houston, Texas. The physician was the most qualified we could find for her type of cancer. We made the trip by automobile, and I accompanied her through the examination and following consultation. The physician conducted the exam and then provided the results to a team of physicians for their review. A prognosis was developed as a result of the review, and the examining physician conducted the consultation. It was not good. The existing treatments were appropriate. I made the mistake of asking what average survival time was expected, and we were told about a year.

In the automobile headed back to Colorado, that was the first time since the initial prognosis, and before her valiant effort to regain strength, that I sensed a somewhat hopeless tone in her voice.

From that time forward, although we continued to travel and enjoy life in Pueblo, there was an awareness in Susie that was not there before. She began telling me we should not be spending the money to do the things we were doing because it was my retirement that we were spending. I reminded her that it was *our* retirement, in terms of both the time and the money being spent. She also began giving me instructions on which women in town could replace her—and more important, which ones could not. This was one of the most difficult things for me to deal with, because whatever response I gave seemed either inadequate or insensitive to me.

Susie continued to tolerate the chemo well, and for the next several months, she thoroughly enjoyed Cowboy. She maintained her strength to continue golfing, and she did not pause in her pursuit of the Irish Tenors. The trips to the oncologist, although never revealing anything alarming, provided little if any encouragement. Her demeanor had changed significantly in the past few weeks, and it reflected a somewhat apathetic approach toward life outside of her little world. Even the holidays passed with little notice. One could not critique any person in her situation for traveling this path, but it was difficult for me to watch her decline. I sobbed often, mostly when commuting to work.

In the fall of 2004, we were walking on a street some distance from our house. We passed a newly built house with a contractor's "for sale" sign in the yard. Susie decided that we should take a look. The builder happened to be working on the nearly finished home and gladly gave us the grand tour. It was probably the closest thing to her dream home that we had ever seen. She lit up as we discussed the house and how we might decorate it. The mortgage on our current residence was relatively small, and we had some accumulated cash. We struck a deal with the builder, and he and his wife became good friends shortly thereafter.

The deal was predicated on selling our current residence in a reasonable period. We called our favorite realtor, who was a friend and associate of mine, and shortly he arrived at our home. While we were reviewing the listing documents, he received a call from an associate who had a client who needed a specific house, and in a hurry. Our realtor's response was, "I'm sitting in it." The other realtor and her clients arrived at our house within twenty minutes, took a reasonable tour of the house, and made an offer. We countered, they accepted, and we had a contract to sell our home prior to signing the listing agreement!

The closing on both homes transpired quickly, and fortunately for us, the builder of the new home allowed me to move a large percentage of our things into the massive garage while he was completing the final touches. A few days before we closed on the previous home, we hired a firm to move our large items for us. The closings took place, and in less than a month, we were in our new accommodations. After that was the chore of setting and arranging furniture and unpacking boxes. This went fairly smoothly, and by the end of November, we had window coverings in, and the place was livable and lovely. We got a Bose sound system and some watercolors of horses by an Evergreen artist whose work Susie admired and from whom Susie had taken watercolor lessons. We celebrated Thanksgiving and Christmas in an enjoyable way, unlike the few previous years.

Then in late December 2004, sometime after Christmas, the phone rang. I was in another room of the house and heard Susie answer, talk for several minutes, and hang up. She immediately began crying. I rushed into the room and tried to console her while attempting to ascertain the cause of her uncontrollable sobbing. She finally was

41

able to talk, and apprised me that Jim Gibbons had called. Jim and his wife, Lila, were close friends from Aspen who had moved to Santa Fe. Lila had unexpectedly died in her sleep the previous night. Jim was surrounded by family and wished me to call the next day.

It is hard to find words in a situation like this. I knew that Susie was thinking the next call would be me, notifying our friends of her death.

I tried, with some success, to engage her in conversation about the past times we'd had together with this special couple and the great memories we had of traveling to horse shows with them. She participated and then seemed to regain her composure. This was a bit of a setback in what had been a very positive few months.

I called Jim the next day, and we lamented together over the phone. Then his strong personality surfaced, and we spoke of other things. I knew he would be fine. Our long-distance friendship was soon to grow into more of a brotherhood.

Chapter 12

$\mathcal{A}$ Sudden End

The next two weeks were spent preparing for a trip to Naples, Florida, to visit friends. Frank and Vickie had moved there from Breckenridge. Around mid-January 2005, we flew there and spent a week exploring the area, playing golf, and eating and drinking with our friends. During our visit, on January 17 we celebrated Susie's sixty-seventh birthday. Toward the end of our stay, other friends from Vail, Colorado, who were staying in an RV park nearby, joined us for lunch. It was an enjoyable few hours of reminiscing about our adventurous days in Ski Country. The next day, it was time to leave for home. During the plane ride to Denver, Susie commented, "Well, at least I made it to sixty-seven."

We arrived home on a Friday at a reasonable hour, and we were able to unpack, grab dinner at a nearby restaurant, and catch a good night's sleep. Before bed, we discussed how well the new house had turned out.

On Saturday morning, we woke well rested, and the phone rang. It was one of the couples with whom we had golfed many times. They were inviting us to play later in the day at the country club. We accepted. Although it was January, the weather was pleasant, and we had a very enjoyable round. We had a few drinks and dinner with our friends, and then we proceeded home to prepare for the coming week. Susie had not received her chemo treatments for over a week, and we were anxious to resume.

We retired at a reasonable hour and promptly fell to sleep. About midnight, I once again woke to her screaming due to unbearable abdominal pain. I dressed quickly, gathered her things, and rushed her to the emergency room. As I had submitted a rather abrasive letter to the hospital's CEO regarding her previous experience with the emergency personnel, they quickly administered to her.

With rather impressive efficiency, she was moved into the examination area, examined with x-ray or some other means, and diagnosed with an abdominal obstruction. She was quickly fitted with a tube through her nose and down her esophagus to extract, as well as to prevent the buildup of the digestive substance causing her discomfort. This process of getting her admitted and finally being settled into the hospital room took well into Sunday.

She was very uncomfortable, as anyone would be with a tube inserted in such a way. I was more concerned for her than I had ever been. I did all I could to try to comfort her mentally and physically for the next several hours. Nighttime came and went. There was little sleep for either of us.

Morning arrived, and with it came the most important visitor: Barry, our friend and doctor. He would provide more encouragement and reassurance through the course of this event than any other person. During the day, the surgeon who had performed her initial procedure visited and informed us that she would require immediate surgery to remove a part of her intestine, and thus the obstruction. Surgery was scheduled for early the following day.

Following the procedure, the surgeon called me into a room. I requested that three friends who'd sat with me the entire time join us. It was a very small room, and we all stood while he informed me that the operation accomplished its purpose. She should survive the trauma, but Susie would tolerate no further surgery. Chemotherapy should extend her life, but any further, such occurrences would be fatal.

The emptiness in my stomach bordered on nausea. Our friends consoled me, and because it would be some time before Susie would regain consciousness, they took me to lunch. I had little appetite, but knew I must sustain myself because there was a major challenge ahead.

I remember little of the next two days. One thing that does come to mind—and not in a pleasant way—was that after her necessary time in the recovery room, Susie was transferred to a hospital room in a section next to an area that was under renovation. The workers were using saws made for cutting steel, and they made ear-shattering clamor that was unbearable for those of us who were healthy. God only knows what it was doing for the patients who had just undergone surgery. I attempted to have the administration either put a stop to the noise or move Susie to another section of the hospital, to no avail.

Barry arrived at a time when the noise was temporarily mute, and I was about to inform him of the issue when the racket resumed. He said not a word but headed directly to the nurse's station. Although I could not hear any of what was said, it was obvious that he was having a somewhat heated discussion. It was evident that the discussion was ineffective, and Barry ended it by grabbing a nearby phone, holding a one minute-conversation, and returning to Susie's room. Within two minutes, her bed was wheeled onto an elevator and to the section of the hospital that was the farthest from the area being renovated. I never asked him whom he called or what he said, and he never volunteered the information.

Susie was miserable, communicated little, and showed no signs of a will to live. I remained with her constantly, and then late on Thursday afternoon, January 27, 2005, she demanded that the catheter be removed because she had an extremely strong urge to urinate. The nurses entered the room and checked the urine reservoir, which had been emptied some time ago and remained empty. I feared that her kidneys had ceased to function. There was a rush to bring diagnostic equipment into the room to determine whether the catheter had malfunctioned. It had not. Her bladder was empty. It was then that I noticed her color had changed to a ghastly yellow. She began talking more than she had in days, saying strange things and joking with the nurses, even when they were seriously informing her that she was very ill.

I knew that her mind was being affected by whatever was happening. Suddenly Barry appeared, and I knew that this was a moment of reckoning. Susie was now lying calmly in the bed and talking to him. Her conversation was incoherent. Barry did a thorough examination. By now, she appeared to be unconscious. I pulled a chair to her bedside and sat holding her hand, not knowing what to do. No one does in this situation. Barry retreated from the room and stood outside the door, where he could observe. It was suddenly clear there was nothing more that could be done.

Just then, Stan Herman, who had called earlier to say he was dropping by, appeared at the doorway. He saw what was transpiring and began to retreat. I called to him quietly and asked that he join me in the room. I truly did not want to be alone through this. With just a brief pat on the shoulder, he moved to a chair well in the back of the room. Susie began to clap her hands and smile while mumbling incoherently. I could not help but think that in these final moments, she was with the Irish Tenors in concert.

Barry entered the room and briefly checked her vitals. He exited quickly and quietly.

Although not labored, her breathing became more and more shallow. She continued the applause and the smile, however the mumbling was now only a movement of her lips. I suddenly realized that I was caressing her forehead as I held her hand, and I had been since this began.

Susie's breathing became so weak that I could barely detect it. Then all motion ceased, the smile left her face, and she froze in a rather peculiar position. She was gone. At some point during this time, the door to the room had been closed. I had not noticed. I picked up the patient signaling device, called the nurse's station, and asked that Barry come in. He confirmed what I had feared for over three years: Susie had left me. I kissed Susie's forehead and whispered, "I love you, man," a phrase from a movie that we had seen together and that became our primary means of expressing our love for each other. I was now alone.

I had cried my eyes red so many times over the past many months that I couldn't believe there were tears left to weep now, but they came. I was hugged by Barry, the nurses, and another person or two whom I did not know.

I gathered Susie's things from the room and departed as soon as I was certain that the proper arrangements had been made to transport her from the hospital. Stan and I walked together from the hospital to the parking garage, where I stowed everything in my van and got into his pickup. Cowboy remained at the kennel over the weekend of our return from Florida, and with this turn of events, he remained there. I asked Stan to take me somewhere for a good, stiff drink. I was not in denial, but I had not quite grasped what had happened.

Stan called his wife, Cindy, who met us at an Applebee's near their home. We had a couple of drinks and dinner, and we pondered all of the things facing me over the next several days. The "me" became "us" for these wonderful friends. They offered their guest room to me that night, and I accepted. There was no way I wanted to enter our house at that point.

The next couple of days are somewhat of a blur. The next morning, Stan hustled me into his vehicle and drove directly to the country club, where he insisted that we play nine holes of golf to settle our thoughts. It was a grand idea. We walked and talked some, but mostly we let our feelings emerge. There was much to do in a short period of time: arrangements with the mortuary, placement of an obituary, notification of family and close friends, and planning a gathering of a small group of close friends to remember Susie. We finished the golf, and Stan accompanied me to the mortuary, where I made arrangements for cremation. With lunch occurring somewhere along the way, we ended up at the kitchen table in Stan's and Cindy's home. Cindy found a picture of Susie, which brought tears to all of our eyes, and the three of us coauthored an obituary for publication. With this delivered, I felt it necessary to relieve them of their therapeutic duties. It was time to go home.

.

Chapter 13

What Friends Do

I left Cowboy in the kennel because I had much to consider over the coming weekend. It was very strange to enter the house where Susie had been alive and vibrant less than a week before. Tears swelled frequently as I tried to adjust to my situation. Although I knew this day would come, I guess I continued to assume that something would block its inevitability.

Beautiful window coverings that she had painstakingly chosen, and which I had already begun to take for granted, now jumped out at me, shaking me violently. The space on the living area floor where she had chosen to place a new couch, and which we had decided to put off purchasing until our return from Florida, now became a focal point. Each time I entered the room, that space suddenly echoed her discussions as to how it should be adorned. It was as if she were there in the room with me. Reality then returned, and the tears began.

That night, I was so exhausted that I slept without waking. However, I had numerous dreams, each with Susie as she had been in her healthy state, and each containing very realistic adventures or incidents we had experienced in real life. It was as if none of the past three-plus years had occurred. Then I awoke and again reality returned. My heart sank to new depths. I broke down for the first and final time. The dreams, although less intense, would return for possibly the rest of my life, but that was the last total emotional collapse I would experience. That one event was almost impossible to bear, but ultimately it was more therapy than could have been provided by any other means. Thereafter, those dreams kept memories of our most cherished times alive, and they moved me from dreading them to embracing them. I continue to think fondly of Susie every day, and I will throughout my life.

Until this moment, I had not known what loneliness was. I had no interest in outside inspiration, and I had no one to turn to. I needed a distraction, and for whatever reason, I stepped into our walk-in closet. There was her entire expanse of clothes. Susie had passed away on Thursday afternoon, and it was now Saturday morning. She had instructed me to take her entire wardrobe to a local resale store, and to direct them to forward all monies obtained to the spay and neuter clinic to which she had donated innumerable hours and dollars. I guess I had decided that I needed something to do, that fulfilling this directive was not going to become easier with time.

I opened the rear of one of the vans, removed the seats, and began hauling clothes. I carefully laid them on the floor of the vehicle until it was stacked full, from end to end and floor to roof. Whatever was left, I stuffed onto the front passenger seat. I took my position at the wheel, opened the garage door, and drove into the pouring rain on my way to a secondhand clothing store. I then negotiated with the manager to sell what she could, forward the proceeds from sales as Susie had directed, and give the remaining items to charity. She agreed. I hauled the entire load into the rear of the store through the rain, helped the manager hang the clothes, and was soon on my way.

I know that many people who lose a spouse of many years (our thirty-eighth anniversary was two weeks away) often have difficulty removing personal items, sometimes for many years. In looking back,

I believe that the longer those items remain, the more comfortable the survivor feels with them—and the harder it is to part with them because the presence of those items replaces the presence of the person. I was fortunate. That one decision seemed to set me on a course of letting go. As previously mentioned, I had mourned my loss of Susie for the past few years, and more intensely over the past two days. Now I was turning from tangible items, which to me prolonged the unhappy and sometimes self-pitying part of this process, to recalling memories, some distant and some more current, but all of which brought a sense of comfort and happiness to me. I had a very long period ahead of me to deal with loneliness and emptiness, but I could now face it with her through fond memories, rather than in a dark, depressing, self-absorbed way in a house full of her things.

Late that morning, I retrieved Cowboy from the kennel, and we had a grand homecoming celebration. I don't remember his being so excited about seeing me, even following some of our longer journeys. When he spotted me, he rushed directly at me from the front and threw his forepaws upon my shoulders. We actually embraced, and I received a face full of poodle tongue. That embrace would become a daily ritual every time I entered the house, until Cowboy and I parted. I hurried us home, and he ran around the house looking for Susie. He charged out the doggie door and into the expansive back yard, circling it many times before returning to the inside. It was obvious he was greatly disappointed. There was nothing to be done to help him understand.

I had notified John Harris, a close friend from Texas, of Susie's passing on Friday. To my surprise, he called Saturday and informed me that he was flying in within the next couple of days to spend some time with me. I was delighted. John was the corporate attorney for the companies I had worked for in Texas, and we had teamed well together within the organizations. In many ways he was a mentor, although he was somewhat younger than I. John and his family had become our closest friends in Texas. We had spent much time golfing and even partying some, and we had visited back and forth many times since our move back to Colorado. His staying for a few days would be just the support I needed.

Maybe he will answer the door occasionally when the members of the Casserole Brigade drop by, I thought. These well-meaning people were a little more than I could tolerate at times, and I often retreated to the master suite and darkened the rest of the house, or I stayed out a bit later for dinner to avoid their arrivals. (I will address this group a little further on.)

On Friday, I had also notified Jim Gibbons in Santa Fe that I had lost Susie, and he and I tried to visit as we sobbed over our recent heartbreaks.

Although it had been just a short time, on Monday I returned to work. as I had not stepped into the bank for over a week, and I'd had little contact during that time. It was a difficult time. Our group was rather close-knit for a business, and there were plenty of hugs and tears. As would be expected, everything was running smoothly, and I spent a short day returning home to prepare for John's arrival. I did contact the holding company staff and members of the board of directors to notify them and to check in.

John arrived and stayed for about a week. It was timely. The next thing that needed to be addressed was Susie's wish that no memorial service be held. Instead, she preferred an informal gathering of close golfing friends. John helped in every way imaginable, driving to pick things up, cleaning, and keeping me on a somewhat even keel, which was not easy at this particular time.

Although there were many people (some from out of town) who I felt would be hurt if they were not made aware of the gathering, I stuck with Susie's wishes and invited about twenty-five people. One of these was Roy Gillmore. He had been involved with me in all of the Western Colorado banks over a period of about fifteen years. As well as being my right arm professionally, he was a learned cowboy and horseman. He and Susie had developed a relationship of friendship and respect through horses that was highly unusual. Roy is like a brother to me, and I believe he was the same to Susie. He was now a senior officer with one of our affiliated banks, and he had been an enormous factor in Susie's quality of life during the final months.

Stan and Cindy helped with all phases of the gathering, from informing those who were invited to supplying refreshments and organizing appetizers, many of which were brought by those attending. Stan brought his stash of booze, which when combined with mine was more than adequate for the occasion. They made certain that the gathering was organized, and of course Stan led the group in a round robin of remembrances of Susie. Although I had dreaded this event, it turned out to be a warm and memorable experience—in spite of the gentleman who drank Stan's entire bottle of twelve-year-old scotch. He and his inebriated wife, neither of whom could walk nor talk, had to be chauffeured home.

Chapter 14

Sad and Final Goodbye

The gathering was behind me. John had shored me up and returned to Texas. Stan and Cindy were back to their normal routine. It was now time for me to develop my routine and try to move forward.

I had no idea how lost in this world one could feel as a result of losing one's closest companion. I discovered that my entire married life had been devoted to us. Although I carried tremendous responsibility throughout my career, I was incredibly focused on our relationship, our security, and our happiness. It had been a partnership through all of this, including my career, and now I had no one with whom to discuss all of my personal thoughts and actions. There was no one who would be affected by those thoughts and actions. I became very lonely in a different way.

I was quick to deal with the physical part of being alone—maybe because I had prepared for it during these past few years, and maybe because I had Cowboy—but I was at a loss when it came to dealing with this subliminal occurrence. I suddenly questioned my devotions to the bank, the community, and even to my friends. I felt like a loose helium balloon, floating on the air currents with absolutely no control, and definitely with no flight plan or destination. It was the worst part of the emptiness. I would arrive home from work, golf, or a community meeting, my mind loaded with things that I would have been anxious to drop on Susie. Although it was better than speaking to a wall, Cowboy understood little of what I was unloading.

I look back on my many thoughts at that time and wonder what would have happened if I had quit my job, sold everything, and hit the road in a Corvette, on an adventure following the historical Route 66. I was sixty-four, and I am sure that two weeks into that trip, I would have had some serious regrets. I also considered quitting my job and moving to Montrose, Colorado, where I would become a fly-fishing junkie. I am guessing that in either case, I would have spent more time in saloons and honky-tonks than fishing or driving the famed route.

I walked through the house one day and performed a mental inventory. I suddenly realized that there were many items that had been in Susie's family for countless years. Among them were silver, china, antique furniture, and three or four oriental rugs. Susie had no siblings back in Minnesota, but she did have a cousin who, like her, had moved to Denver shortly after college. He was now retired and living in Albuquerque. He had a daughter in the Denver area and a son in Santa Fe. Many of these items dated back to their grandparents, and some were from Susie's cousin's father. I decided that I would invite them to come and choose whatever they desired from the collection. I did so, and they all arrived one weekend. Thankfully, they were interested in most of the items.

A couple of pieces of the furniture were too large to fit in the vehicle belonging to the son from Santa Fe, and I volunteered to throw them into the van and deliver them to him.

Susie had put our poodle Boomer's ashes in one of the closets in our new home, and I had placed hers alongside. During our marriage,

Susie's mother's poodle, which we adopted after her death, and Boomer were like children to Susie. She had a relationship with both dogs, and later with Cowboy, that I believe replaced the children we never had. We had buried her mother's dog on our property next to the golf course when we had lived near Austin. Since she had only requested that she be allowed to return to the natural state with the earth after her death, I decided to spread both Susie's and Boomer's ashes on the golf course in Austin, next to the burial site of her mother's poodle. I called John in Austin and scheduled to drive there for this purpose; I'd also spend a few days visiting.

Soon I was on my way. I took a minimal detour through Santa Fe to drop off the furniture to Susie's relative and spend the night with Jim Gibbons. We went out to dinner and retired early, because I had a long day of driving ahead of me the next day, and the weather did not look favorable. It was late February, as I recall, and there was always the possibility of winter storms.

I woke the next morning to gray skies that spat a few snowflakes. I had delivered the furniture the previous day and was able to get on the road rather early. I chose to take US Highway 285 south of Santa Fe for about forty-five miles to connect with Interstate 40, which would take me east into Texas. This allowed my avoiding congestion in Albuquerque.

About five miles east of Santa Fe on Interstate 25, I began to see spots of ice along the edges of the road. I reached the exit for US 285 south, and shortly after departing the interstate, I noticed ice on the traffic lanes. This soon became thick, glaring ice that made driving slow and treacherous.

It took about two hours to reach Clines Corners, where US 285 intersects Interstate 40. I stopped because the stress of the drive had triggered several incentives to do so. It should be noted that Jim

Gibbons called me about the time I reached the ice outside of Santa Fe—and about every fifteen minutes thereafter—to ascertain that I was not belly-up in a field somewhere. Although traffic had not been heavy, there were numerous vehicles in various stages of disarray alongside the road. Once I was eastbound on Interstate 40, the ice dissipated rather rapidly, and the remainder of the trip to Austin was without incident.

John was the perfect host and volunteered to assist me with the ashes. We had a rather pleasant evening with dinner out. The next morning, we were scheduled to spread the ashes. I was not very comfortable about this because I was going to leave the last physical link to my love of thirty-eight years, and my favorite animal of all time, scattered on the cold earth, 850 miles from home. Without my asking, John had retrieved a bucket and scoop from his garage. We loaded them into the van and were on our way to Bastrop, Texas, and the Pine Forest Golf Club.

Just after leaving John's home, it began to rain. This continued for the balance of the day. We arrived at the golf course about an hour later and entered the clubhouse. I explained to the person behind the counter that I had lived on the first fairway, and that I would like to spread my wife's ashes and those of our poodle who had romped with her on the course near our former home. He could not have been more accommodating. He indicated that because it was raining, there would be no concern of our disrupting play on the course, and he offered us a golf cart to use. We took the bucket out of the van, emptied both containers of ashes into the bucket, mixed them, and headed to the golf course with the scoop.

With a breeze blowing and light rain falling, I stood on the fairway in exactly the spot I had pictured; John stood a distance behind. I began sprinkling the ashes from side to side onto the wet turf. It seemed for a while that the bucket would never empty, and then suddenly there was nothing left. The entire time tears ran down my cheeks, and but for the red eyes, no one would have noticed the tears because the rain drops were camouflaging them. I turned to John, and I think I smiled. I scattered the remnants from the bucket, and we left.

The memories and thoughts that passed through my mind in that short time were like a lifetime reduced to a very few minutes. I felt that I had fulfilled Susie's request but not left her alone, and I'd found some peace for myself for the first time in over three years.

John later mentioned that when I turned back toward him, he saw relief in my expression.

Chapter 15

Further Tragedy

I was back in Colorado. Cowboy's companionship was fantastic medicine. We walked three to five miles virtually every day. All day long while I worked, he had run of the house and the yard, and after those long morning walks, he was very contented. Between my full days at the bank and his company at home, my loneliness was slowly retreating, but not the emptiness.

Somewhere around March, I received a call from Bob Sterling. Bob and his wife, Suzy, were close friends of ours during the Aspen years and beyond. Bob and I had fished thousands of hours together both in Colorado, and in the blue ribbon waters of Wyoming, Montana, and Idaho. The four of us had traveled together, dined together, camped together, and shared many other adventures. Bob and I had also played a fair amount of golf. He played golf not unlike a pro, whereas I struggled along behind. We always had fun. He is a musician and an accomplished architect, and he co-authored *Angling Guides* with the late Chuck Fothergill, who was a well-known fly fishing authority, and whom I also counted among my friends. Although they now reside in Bozeman, Montana, Bob and Suzy remain dear friends.

This call was unexpected and timely. Bob and seven of his golfing buddies from Aspen had arranged a golfing tour of Scotland in May, only sixty days away. One of the eight had a situation that forced him to withdraw from the trip. I was invited to take his place. I accepted immediately because I knew all but one of the group, and I really did need to remove myself from the bombardment of well-meaning folks expressing sympathy. At first it was comforting, but in a short time, I found myself avoiding contact with others as much as possible. If they were uncomfortable finding the appropriate words—and it was often obvious that they were—they could not have imagined how difficult it was for me to fashion a suitable response.

The Scotland trip was an eye-opener for me. I had traveled domestically on frequent occasions, both flying and driving, but this first trip abroad was just what I needed to divert my thoughts from recent events. My brother Ron lived a reasonable distance from Denver International Airport, and he allowed me to stay overnight before leaving. He then drove me to the airport the following morning and dropped me off there. I met the group, and we boarded without incident.

Our first leg to Dulles International Airport was a cakewalk for a seasoned traveler such as me. We then transferred to the international flight and headed to London Heathrow Airport. The flight across was longer than any I had flown before, and due to the nonstop, louder-than-necessary conversationalists; the nearby snorer, who sounded as though someone was writing on a blackboard with a pickle; and my having to follow the flight's location on the monitor on the seatback in front of me, I got little sleep during the eight-hour flight.

I had never experienced anything like Heathrow. We collected our baggage and golf clubs and deposited them in trolley carts, which we pushed through shoulder-to-shoulder crowds. We traveled through seemingly endless, actually stark, and ever-crowded hallways. When the hallways did end, they entered huge, cavernous rooms that were packed with more people trying to choose the correct hallway out of the many.

The people with whom I was traveling had all indicated that they had much experience at this, but they took us to places from which we must backtrack to get on course. I think there was some construction going on. It seemed as if we traveled ten miles to finally reach customs. Here, the lines were staggering, but the process was efficient. We soon passed through, rechecked our bags, and were on our way to Edinburgh.

It's been so long that I do not remember the names of the towns in which we stayed, or the golf courses that we played, but I can certainly remember my two favorite things about Scotland. First up was the people, and then there was the whiskey! As eight men in their sixties and on a golf outing in Scotland might do, we sampled a number of pubs in this fascinating country. Each smoke-filled, low-ceilinged, dim-lighted den that we entered was filled with happy folks eager to meet us and include us in the evening's merriment. We most often answered their questions about Colorado, and it seemed that of all the places that they would visit if given the opportunity to travel in the US, Colorado and California were at the top of the list.

It seemed that there was a distillery about every five miles along our routes. We toured some, but most often were able to get a good sampling of the products of nearby distillers in the pubs located in the villages where we stayed. The many flavors of these whiskeys were beyond anything I might have imagined. The now waning peat-fired stills, the wood cask types, and the aging processes were enlightening for someone who had no familiarity with the methods used to create these highly sought-after tonics.

The golf was spectacular, the weather was puzzling, and the travel was frightening. We had rented two minivans, and the person whose names in which they were contracted were the only ones allowed to drive. Chuck was our driver. Chuck has been a valued friend over the years, but I must say I hope that I never have an opportunity to be his passenger again. He enjoyed narrating and pointing out the many interesting historical and geographic marvels along the way. Unfortunately, one drives on the left side of the road in the UK, and the folks there tend to drive the narrow and curvy roads rather speedily. Chuck often reverted to the American side of the road, and when awakened by the blaring of numerous horns, he would bounce off the curb on the left side of the road during the correction process. These events were only surpassed in passenger anxiety by his skill at negotiating the many roundabouts through which we passed. Most of these we entered once again in the right lane, and we were fortunate to exit at all, let alone at the correct street. We did survive Chuck, and we enjoyed the entire experience.

The last stop on our golfing itinerary was the Old Course at St. Andrews, the birthplace of the game. We had stayed at a resort the night before leaving for St. Andrews. The place had separate cabins, one of which Bob and I shared. It also had a pub connected to the dining room, where a whiskey tasting was scheduled for that evening, and we attended. Midway through the tasting, I was interrupted by the desk clerk with a message to call the bank. For my staff to interrupt me on a trip such as this meant only one thing: important, and probably bad, news. It was both. My friend and boss had committed suicide. My heart sank. I was on a therapeutic trip to ease the heartache of my recent loss, and now there was another tragedy.

I drank more than my share of Scotch that night and retired. I slept little, and at first thing in the morning, I bid farewell to my friends. I contacted the airline and was fortunate to be connected to the most patient and helpful person who'd ever graced an air carrier's customer service telephone. I booked a return flight home that day from Edinburgh, and now my only problem was getting there. I was about two hours away, and when I approached the resort desk, I was told there was really no public transportation available. After much discussion with the clerks, the manager emerged from her office. She was a woman of about fifty, and she was pleasant and quite attractive. She had a solution: she would drive me. She packed me and my baggage into her auto, and we were off. I enjoyed the most pleasant conversation that I had participated in for years. If it had not been for the tragic circumstances, I would have canceled that flight and returned to the resort with her, just to extend that moment in time. I offered to pay her for the ride, but she would have no part of it. She only asked that I promise to visit if I were ever able to return.

With the many things now running through my mind, it seemed as if the three legs of the return trip, the second Heathrow experience, and passing through customs at Dulles International were a short, blurred dream. I suddenly found myself back at Denver International Airport, with my brother Ron picking me up at the curb.

My life had now taken a new turn. It was only four months since I'd lost Susie, and I was an honorary pallbearer at a funeral. It is always a difficult thing to lose a friend, but when that person takes his own life, it is from a different viewpoint. There was nothing I could do for Susie, but could I have helped prevent my friend's loss? I knew there were issues, and I did make attempts to be closer to him. They seemed fruitless, but maybe I gave up too soon. These things all passed through my mind. The important thing was to let them pass. One must not let those thoughts linger.

It was not long after the service that those of us in the management structure of the holding company were called upon to make a number of critical decisions. For tax reasons, the end result was that the banks would need to be sold, the holding company would need to be disbanded, and all proceeds of the Employee Stock Ownership Plan would need to be distributed. This was a difficult time because I was sixty-three years old, and I could dimly see the end of my career in the fog ahead.

Over the next year, there were numerable meetings regarding the task at hand, and all of this further complicated my life, which was already as if someone had tossed it into a Mixmaster and set it on puree. I was traveling to meetings in Denver more frequently, trying to determine what to do with my large house, which I used little and which was somewhat barren of furniture, and setting my bank on a course of preparing and staging for sale. Fortunately, we had excellent legal representation, a cohesive holding company board of directors, and a well-positioned product to offer. These banks were clean, profitable, and located in growing markets.

Chapter 16

Casserole Brigade

I was fortunate. I had several local friends who contributed to my moving forward from what might have been a very dark period in my life.

Jim Gibbons and I visited each other frequently to play golf and discuss our comparable situations, particularly while he remained in Santa Fe. We invited one another to our respective homes, and we would spend a couple of days golfing, drinking moderately (or more), and often introducing each other to our local friends who had similar interests. This was a valuable diversion because it moved both of us away from the familiar and helped wrest us from the all-too easy syndrome of hanging out at home and avoiding outside contact. I'm not sure that he had a problem with that, but I certainly did.

Later, Jim moved from Santa Fe back to the Aspen area, and although our visits continued, they were less frequent.

Roy Gillmore called frequently, and he also met me for cocktails or dinner each time he passed through town with time to spare. We discussed many things from our past together, banking, the communities, many people whose paths we had crossed, and Susie. All of this was very helpful. In addition, we also discussed some of our private and professional issues. This had occurred previously, when we dealt with the highs and lows of our banking experiences.

Darrell Neu, who owned a waste disposal company and was also an accomplished auctioneer, provided additional support. He joined me for breakfast or lunch several days a week. A few years before, he had mentored me through a rather mediocre attempt at becoming an auctioneer, and on several occasions he allowed me to join him on stage and chant away. He always told me that he needed the help, but looking back, I believe he took pity on the old man. Most important, he also provided the ear on which I frequently needed to unload daily frustrations and concerns.

Stan Herman had apparently had difficulties with his marriage for some time and about a year after my finding myself living alone he became separated. Stan moved from their spacious home in Pueblo to a small apartment in Pueblo West that was actually one-half of a duplex. He brought little more than his BMW motorcycle and the clothes that he wore. Stan's new digs were about two miles from my home and, because he had sparse furniture, no view, and barely enough room to stretch and yawn in, he often gravitated to my place. He actually referred to his new quarters as the hovel. It was not a bad description.

The result of this proximity was our counseling one another on many things such as culinary arts, the finer points of the aged and not-so-aged spirits, men's fashion, how to live in Pueblo, the pros and cons of Sonic versus Dairy Queen, beer, grinders, and how to deal with an unknown future.

Stan and I spent many a lunch together, and we ate dinner out a few nights a week. Darrell and I joined each other for breakfast also a few times a week, and the three of us in varying combinations spent many a night in the neighborhood restaurants and bars. I seemed to be the common denominator in that last category. I can't say that I developed a drinking problem, but I certainly developed a palate for a more than occasional gin, wine, or beer. Roy Gillmore would also occasionally stop by the bars.

Now, returning to the casserole brigade, this was initially several individuals approaching my door soon after my loss and bringing food of various sizes and shapes, as well as other well-meant offerings to help me get through a difficult period. Most of these donors were women, and so my guy friends somehow put the thought in my head that I had become a very eligible bachelor, and that there were motives other than my well-being involved.

I dismissed that theory until the first phone call came from a neighbor who had invited me to dinner with a couple who had been longtime friends of theirs. It was only a few months after my being widowed. I had attended the dinner and had a very enjoyable time. The other couple had some things in common with me, and as a result, we communicated comfortably all evening. Less than a week later, the neighbor called and, obviously being very uncomfortable, asked if I were dating yet. I responded that I had not really even thought of it. She was very apologetic and revealed that the other couple, after I had left the evening of the dinner, had coerced her into calling. They had a single friend who they felt was a good match. She even rode a Harley.

I politely informed her that I had no interest in meeting anyone. I then asked her to thank the others for thinking of me. I didn't have the heart to tell her that I thought people who rode Harleys were placed on this earth to get their enjoyment from applying unbearable decibels of racket upon my eardrums, and that had their parents afforded them more attention as children, they would likely not feel the need to draw such attention through agonizing entire neighborhoods with their din.

That call did begin a thought process for me. I truly had not considered dating. I had mentioned to some of my friends that I had no interest in another relationship because I could not bear the thought of losing someone else. I was not sure that I could survive it again myself. After that call and careful consideration, that became my mindset.

In spite of my resistance, there seemed to be an urgency on the part of female suitors and their agents. There were business owners, business managers, waitresses, and school teachers, to name a few. I quickly exhausted my rather bleak list of responses to these folks. Some of them came directly at me, but most were represented by well-meaning friends, some of who I didn't even know were my friends.

The people caught up in this stampede whom I had great pity for were the friends of mine who were husbands or partners of women trying to attach their friends to my life. In one instance, a close friend and valued bank customer felt compelled to advocate for a friend of his companion who I knew had played golf with Susie, but whom I didn't recall having ever met. He brought her name up virtually every time we met, whether playing golf or in business meetings. I had no interest in this woman, and I thought that I had made that clear, at least in a subtle way. The barrage continued.

One day I happened to stop in alone at one of my favorite restaurants for a quiet lunch. I ordered and was sitting, contemplating probably nothing, when the owner approached and sat across from me in the booth. He felt obliged to enlighten me of an occurrence at his bar the previous evening. My friend's companion and the woman (who couldn't understand no) had been at the bar having a cocktail. He had overheard them actually planning a strategy for getting the two of us together. The restaurant owner exclaimed, "I'll bet you're getting a lot of that lately. Do you know this woman? If I were you, I would run like hell!" I was in no position to run.

Sometime later, I was sitting at the bar in another restaurant, waiting to meet someone for a dinner meeting. This woman approached me, introduced herself, and stated, "I believe we are supposed to have dinner one of these evenings." I was dumfounded and kind of wished I had run like hell.

Most others were not as tenacious, but the whole thing did become an issue that diminished my feeling of intimacy with this city.

Chapter 17

Blue Mustang

Around August 2005, both Roy Gillmore and Stan Herman took exception to my mode of transportation. I believe Stan's was a reference to my two "soccer mom mobiles" and how they would negatively affect my social life. At this point, I was not particularly concerned about my social life, but he continued with, "If you don't get rid of them, you may never get laid again." That got my attention! I had said that I did not want to enter another serious relationship, not that I wanted to become celibate.

At almost the same time, during a conversation on another subject, Roy Gillmore suggested that I look at a new Ford Mustang GT convertible. It was 2005, and that year Ford had released its new retro version of the popular Mustang. I did not know it at the time, but after making a business call on a dealership, he had seen one and discussed it with a female salesperson. He thought that she might catch my eye while elevating my macho status by putting me into a sexier vehicle.

I wasn't aware that he had a specific person in mind to demonstrate the auto, and the concept was not of particular interest to me at that moment, so I cheerfully set that notion aside. Then one Saturday afternoon, on my way home from the bank, I was passing the

Ford dealership in Pueblo. I recalled the conversation with Roy, quickly crossed two lanes of traffic without causing any particular panic among the drivers behind me, and took a quick left into the dealership.

I was met by a middle-aged salesperson with whom I was familiar, told him my story, and was soon reviewing his inventory of Mustang convertibles. I was not picky about engine size, and so I looked at only six-cylinder, basic vehicles, one of which I took on a test drive on US Highway 50 west of town. It was a beautiful fall day, and with the top down, it reminded me of the several years I had spent as a bachelor back in the sixties when I was examining banks and had purchased a new Chevy Impala convertible each year.

This particular car was blue with a tan top, and although I had enjoyed the ride immensely, I had not fallen in love. I thanked the salesman, and as I was leaving, he said, "Let me show you the GT. I have one right outside the door, and it wouldn't be right for you to consider a purchase without seeing it." I agreed, and we stepped out to visually inspect the vehicle. It was a light metallic blue with a black top, and as I gazed almost longingly, he explained all of the standard goodies that were included, one of which was the 300-horsepower V8 engine that developed a rumble from the tailpipes remindful of the sound that had emanated from my 1952 Oldsmobile 98 coupe, which happened to be the fastest car in Alliance, Nebraska, around the time I'd graduated from high school. I did not drive the GT right then, but I told him I would think about it and get back with him on Monday.

I dreamed about that automobile that night. I arose Sunday morning, had breakfast, and drove to the dealership. It was closed on Sundays, but I could get into the lot, and three times that day, I gazed at, caressed, and had an insatiable urge to drive that car. I was deathly afraid that someone had looked at it after I had left the previous day;

maybe someone had purchased it. Believe it or not, I worried about that all that day and Sunday night.

On Monday I arose early, grabbed my checkbook, went to the bank to clear a few things off my desk, and arrived at the dealership the minute the salesroom opened. My salesperson would not be in for an hour. I waited!

Now, one would think that a sixty-four-year-old person could handle this situation in a more mature manner. After all, if someone had purchased that vehicle, couldn't the factory assemble another identical to it and have it delivered in a relatively short period of time? No! There was something special about this particular hunk of steel and plastic.

My man arrived. The car was available! In short order, he had the top down and had reviewed the basic functions with me. I was quickly on Highway 50, once again headed west with the wind swirling about me. The acceleration was invigorating, and that bass reverberation from those tailpipes was akin to listening to golden oldies on the radio. After about a twenty-minute cruise, I was back in the office of the dealership. I worked the salesman pretty hard, and finally the owner came out and said that he was handing me the final offer. He wanted me to own that car, and he was barely covering commissions on the deal. Of course I believed him and wrote a check. Another life-changing event for Harv!

The next day, I drove the car to the bank and parked, top down, in my customary spot in an empty lane of our drive-through area. I went directly to my desk without comment. One of the drive-through tellers noticed the car and asked another if she knew to whom it might belong. After a bit of sleuthing, they determined it was mine. The first teller's remark was, "Here come the bitches!"

Now, I wouldn't exactly describe that vehicle as a babe magnet, but it seemed to have a flair of its own and caught people's eye frequently. I distinctly recall an attractive blonde, who was driving a BMW, followed me all the way from Pueblo to the Wal-Mart in Pueblo West, a distance of about eight miles. She pulled into the parking space next to the Mustang and approached me as I exited the vehicle to proclaim her admiration of the car. She kept me answering questions regarding it for several minutes. I thanked her for her compliments and excused myself to continue into the store. She returned to her car and headed back toward Pueblo. I probably was feeling a little foxy that day, but I got the impression that she might have something on her mind other than throwing kudos at the car. It turns out it was probably all that it was, because I had several such encounters from both male and female admirers of that machine.

It wasn't just a Pueblo thing because it happened in many places nationwide, including a parking area at a trailhead when I was hiking along the Rio Grande Gorge, near Taos, New Mexico; on the ferry on my way to Amelia Island in Florida; and at a trailhead in the Saguaro National Park, near Tucson, Arizona.

One of the most memorable was as I was passing through a town somewhere in the southwest. I was in the right-hand lane on a divided stretch and felt uneasy, as though someone had invaded my space. I had the top down and turned slightly to my left. There was a hand on the top of the car door. Turning a bit further, I was face to face with a gentleman on a Harley. We were moving at maybe thirty-five miles an hour, and he was connected to my vehicle via the grip of this big, hairy hand. He cracked a smile and stated, "I just needed to let you know what a fine-looking automobile you have." I thanked him. He drifted back toward his group, gang, gaggle, or whatever one calls a batch of them riding together. At this point, I seriously wondered whether an individual vehicle could have a special attraction? I had seen several others just like it, so apparently it wasn't unique.

I frequently joined members of the bank's staff for cocktails after work on Friday afternoon. Connie, one of the senior officers, had kind of adopted me after Susie's passing, and she would invite customers or friends of her family. On occasion, she was guilty of inviting some woman who she thought might interest me, or vice versa. I think she proclaimed herself to be the village matchmaker. On one of those evenings, her daughter and another young girl began extolling the virtues of the Mustang. I threw the key to her daughter, and they were off! I thought they would never come back. They did like that ride!

For whatever reason, the purchase of that vehicle made me look at myself differently. To this point in my life, I had lived a structured existence—the career, the marriage, and all of the self-imposed expectations that went with it. What one wore, what one said, what one drove, and where one dined had to be thought through. In a smaller community, one slip of the tongue might negate many marketing dollars.

It never occurred to me that I could own a loud (not as loud as a Harley!), fast muscle car and maybe not offend anyone. It seemed that I had spent my entire adult life trying to please or at least appease everyone. We all know that goal is impossible to achieve.

Chapter 18

A Career Ends

With the coming change in my career path and my recent personal loss, I became more independent. My choice to avoid another committed relationship was now about the only thing to which I was committed. To that, I was steadfast.

I had sensual desires and assumed that at some point, I would attempt to satiate those. For that reason, I began to consider some of the female prospects being cast at me. I actually agreed to meet two or three of them at the after-work cocktail gatherings on Friday evenings. Unfortunately, my interest was soon diminished, and I discovered that I was not emotionally prepared for that step. Maybe I never would be. It was a strange feeling.

I became more of a loner, taking many moderate-length road trips alone. I was more and more uncomfortable being in Pueblo. I had been cast off from all of my business, community service, and social anchors. The banks would be sold. My effectiveness with the 4-H Foundation had run its course, and being single dramatically changed my social environment.

Although I was quite successful at camouflaging it from both myself and others, I was being submerged in self-pity. The trips were made with CDs that Susie and I had shared, resounding from the Mustang's speakers. There were about four of them, and I played them over and over. These major changes in my life had sent me into a spiral into the past, as if I were traveling in a time machine. I only thought of the things that we had done together, and many times I visited the same cities, restaurants, and night clubs where we had fostered pleasant memories.

These recessions allowed me to rationalize my actions. I felt sorry for myself because I had lost or was losing those things that gave my life meaning, including Susie. I remained in mourning. For each person, the time and intensity of this process differs. For me, it would be a couple of years. The things that generated the self-pity were more my not being included in social and business happenings. The banks being on the block was not something that was made public by management, but it became public knowledge by osmosis.

Suddenly, I was not being contacted when seats on boards of community service organizations became vacant. I was not consulted on fundraising issues for different organizations. These were minor things, but the loss of them indicated a diminished stature in a relatively small community. I became depressed that after completion of play in a men's afternoon golf league, following a few drinks, everyone went home to dinner with their families. I felt left out and melancholy. I remember feeling dejected when I was in the car and heading home to be alone. The more I rejected offers from friends and acquaintances to meet single women, the less I got invited to different functions. This was the essence of self-pity. I did not realize all of this at the time, but looking back, it is obvious. I was digging my own hole and would probably pull it in over me given enough time.

Over the next few months, the complexities of the sale of the banks required enough of my time that I was relieved of some of my pessimism, at least during the days. I attended to the bank, for which I was directly responsible, and was present at the holding company meetings where strategies and negotiations took place.

I mentioned earlier that I had assisted Darrell Neu in selling a few charitable auctions, and he was generous, in the sense that he allowed me to do so several times during this period. It was a great distraction for me, and it was probably quite a detraction for the auctions.

It was now early 2006, and it had been over a year since Susie had passed. The sale of two of the banks had been negotiated. The remaining banks were scheduled to close within sixty to ninety days. Through the negotiations for the sale of the bank, for which I was responsible, the bulk of the staff who wished to remain were provided employment. The one exception was me. I was sixty-four, and this bank and its branches would become branches of the acquiring institution. There was no need for a CEO in that scenario. I was offered a ninety-day transitional period and a severance package.

As the time grew closer, I became less enchanted with the thought of sitting in the basement of my old establishment and assuring my loyal customers that all was going to be well under the new ownership. First, I had no guaranty of that myself, and second, this new organization marched to the beat of a new drum that was the opposite of everything in banking philosophy under which I had operated for four and a half decades. The thought of remaining under those circumstances was depressing and nauseating.

Two weeks prior to the closing of the sale, I notified the acquiring management that I would be foregoing my severance package, and that I would resign upon the sale's closing. I remember it well because I was in a waiting room at the hospital, waiting for some now forgotten procedure, when the call I had made to notify them was returned. Even though I was forfeiting a large sum of money, I felt as if a huge weight had been lifted from my shoulders. I now believe that I had made the correct decision.

Chapter 19

Alone

The minute I returned to the bank following the termination of the call that ended my career, I began scheming my plan for the first day after the closing. I was single. I had sufficient resources to do whatever I wanted. I had a Mustang convertible. How about I leave town that day? This became my plan!

I went home that evening and pulled out my State Farm atlas. With the exception of a quick trip to Milwaukee, I had no experience traveling east of the Mississippi, other than flying to Florida and Boston. An extended road trip would be just the ticket.

I commenced the planning process by plotting sites that appealed to me on the US map. My initial plan took me through eastern Colorado, Nebraska, Iowa, Illinois, Indiana, Ohio, Kentucky, Tennessee, a corner of North Carolina, South Carolina, Georgia, Florida and the Keys, Alabama, Mississippi, Louisiana, Texas, New Mexico, and then home. I got quite excited. I wanted to drive reasonable distances on my road days, but I also wanted to spend some time along the way, particularly in Cleveland, Ohio; Charleston, South Carolina; the Florida Keys; Naples, Florida; and Austin, Texas. I calculated about a month to make the trip.

The next two weeks were filled with emotions as I prepared to leave the staff that had taken more than a decade to build. Most had been with me for many years.

Also, as I dealt with these matters, visions of Susie's and my earlier arrival, the struggles to get settled and become a part of this community, and all of the friends we had made over these years continued to surface and bring an empty feeling to my stomach. Some of the folks we had befriended had passed away, some had moved away, and others had moved on. The core group remained, but my contact with them began to diminish over time; our interests took different paths at the frequently arriving forks in the road. This was the final fork.

During the months of arranging for the spin-off of the banks, the process of liquidating the holding company, which would now be a shell of a corporation, was addressed. The primary obligation remaining for the management of the holding company was the disbursement of Employee Stock Ownership Funds to the qualified participants. The most efficient means of accomplishing this was to transfer the funds to a liquidating trust and elect trustees to manage the disbursements. I was named a trustee along with the son of the late controlling owner. This appointment would fill my time following the hiatus I had planned for the extended road trip.

With the assurance that there would be no need for my involvement in the liquidation process until my return, I began packing. It did not take much; the trunk of the Mustang would hold my golf clubs and one small piece of luggage. Everything remaining would tuck around the items in the trunk or find its place on the small rear passenger seat. Following the grief and disappointments that had occurred during the previous eighteen months, I became anxious to embark on a lengthy journey with virtually no responsibility other than to myself. It would be the first time since Susie and I had met thirty-nine years ago.

Chapter 20

Let the Trip Begin

On the day the holding company's management received verification that the closing had occurred and that funds had been received, I believe that I drank rather heavily and then fell asleep. At waking the next morning, a new chapter in my life would begin. I loaded the Mustang, locked up the house, and left Pueblo. The first day, I traveled directly east from the city and then north through eastern Colorado to the small farming community of Brush, where I connected with I-76 eastbound. In just over one hundred miles, I crossed the Nebraska border, at which point I-76 merges with I-80 eastbound. As I passed near Lake McConaughy, Nebraska, I called my sister, Kathy, to let her know I was passing by and to say hello. I had a reservation for the evening in Grand Island, and I did not have time to stop. Besides, I was on a loner trip to avoid long conversations about how I was doing since losing Susie and what I planned to do for the rest of my life.

I had an uneventful evening in Grand Island. A stop anywhere on the I-80 corridor in Nebraska is uneventful, unless you really appreciate a merging of truck stop and carnival atmospheres. At this time, I don't remember where I ate that night. I probably couldn't have told you the next morning.

I woke and rose early on the second day. I wanted to have a short drive into Cleveland, Ohio, on my third day out. Accordingly, I chose to stay in South Bend, Indiana, that evening. It was about seven hundred miles and an eleven-hour drive, but that would give me just under four hours in which to reach Cleveland the following day.

My great friends Brian and Monica Roddy lived in Cleveland, and I wanted to have adequate time to visit them because these rendezvous occurred infrequently. I had worked with Brian during my time in Houston, and Monica visited him there frequently. During that time, I got to know her quite well, and I appreciated her particularly for her ability to remain sane while married to a sizeable and very humorous Irishman.

It was evening when I passed into Indiana. I figured that I was a little over an hour from South Bend, and I was congratulating myself on an arrival that would allow me time to relax, have a couple of drinks and dinner, and get a good night's sleep before heading to Cleveland. It had been a long day. Suddenly there was a plethora of brake lights ahead of me, and automobiles all around had their front bumpers nearly scraping the pavement as the drivers applied maximum brake pressure to stop. Fortunately, there were no collisions, and we all realigned into our respective lanes.

For the next several hours, a ten-mile mass of vehicles moved at the speed of a toll clerk collecting funds from each vehicle. When I finally arrived at the toll station, I was appalled to find that the freeway was under construction and had been narrowed to two lanes rather than the usual five. The state government had made the typically bureaucratic decision to install temporary toll shacks on the remaining two lanes. The poor clerks were under a great deal of duress. It was one of the worst cases of government ineptitude I have ever witnessed. I shall never return to Indiana.

The frustration of the past hours, combined with arriving quite late to my hotel room, negated the drinks, dinner, and relaxation. I had a snacking meal, retired, and hoped for a better day to follow.

The next day, upon the suggestion of the night clerk at the hotel, I took a drive-through tour of the campus at the University of Notre Dame. In my limited exposure to such things, it is one of the most beautiful such campuses existing. I felt that anyone passing through should make the effort to stop.

Brian and Monica had a houseful of children, and so I thought it best if I were to stay at a hotel near their home. They arranged for a room at a nice Holiday Inn, and it was fortunate that it had a bar, because I had a bit of a wait. They were twenty or twenty-five years my junior and were a long stretch from retirement at that time. They arrived after I'd consumed only one Bombay Sapphire on the rocks. Monica immediately inquired of my Mustang. I took them out for a look, and when her eyes lit up, I handed her the keys and suggested that she take it for a spin. She did and was in no hurry to return; Brian and I had at least one healthy cocktail before she returned. Monica was smitten and made it clear that this automobile was on her wish list, with fulfillment anticipated in the not-too-distant future. To this day, I do not know whether it worked out for her, but I'm guessing that if those same thoughts were with her the next morning, it might have happened.

We walked to a nearby steakhouse and were seated at a table with a view of the lightly traveled street outside. Here, the Roddys treated me to a meal that was most gratifying, particularly because I had not enjoyed a normal spread for three days.

Soon after we were seated, a parade of vintage autos appeared on the street below our window, and it lasted for virtually the entire time we were dining. There was a broad spectrum of vehicles. Just when we thought we had seen enough old bangers, something else very interesting came along and renewed our enthusiasm. It made for a very entertaining evening.

This was my first time being totally out of my environment, as well as visiting people with whom I had not had direct contact for a long period of time and with whom I felt close and comfortable. It provided a fresh, new outlook for me. We conversed, laughed, and enjoyed the camaraderie of the evening. We talked of past things in Houston, mostly of a humorous nature, and of current things with them in Cleveland. We touched on their work, play, and many endeavors, and the successes of their children. Little was discussed about my recent life-altering experiences.

I believe this was where I learned to not dwell on past negatives. The experience did validate my feelings that I wanted to pursue the remainder of my life alone. I loved to travel, and I had friends throughout the lower forty-eight. I could pursue golf, fishing, reading, and the yet-to-be-experienced activities that would keep me busy for the rest of my life. I was a loner, the shell was beginning to form around me, and I was comfortable with all of that.

I spent one more day in Cleveland, roaming with Brian through the city. I observed progress in the real estate projects he had been involved in, and I met his landscape company's crew. It was a pleasant relief from being in the car for the many miles I had driven in the past few days. I said my goodbyes and retired for the evening.

Chapter 21

Close Call

The next morning, I proceeded south toward Nashville on Interstates 71 and 65. For many years, I had fostered a strong urge to visit Nashville because classic country music was possibly my favorite genre, and it seemed that a visit to Opryland should be a highlight on a trip such as this.

I arrived at my hotel, which was near Opryland and provided outdoor dining. I had driven for several hours and was rather tired. I checked in, proceeded to the dining room, and was seated in the outdoor area. I remember ordering a sapphire on the rocks and waiting a bit before ordering my meal. During this time, I spoke with one of the restaurant personnel regarding the Opry schedule and what was required to attend one of the weekly performances. After acquiring adequate information, I attempted to plan the evening in my mind.

Suddenly I felt a chill throughout me. Susie was also a fan of classic country music, and she should be with me for this. The feeling would not subside, and tears came to my eyes. I sat there for some time, reflecting. This was the first time in decades that I was without the stress of my career and was doing something that was purely for my relaxation and enjoyment. I thought of the past few years of Susie's life, and how personally stressful it had been for her. She had also shared the stress of my career over those many years. Fate had robbed her of the part of life that I was now enjoying. That night I was unable to attend the Grand Ole Opry. Since then, I've realized that I am thankful for every day, and for everything in my life.

The next morning, I departed early because my destination was Charleston, South Carolina. The trip was about six hundred miles, and I had planned a route that should take around nine hours. My route along I-40 took me through Knoxville to Ashville, North Carolina, and then to I-26 into Charleston. Just before reaching the Appalachian Mountains, I noticed a shack next to a river with a big, not-too-well-engineered sign proclaiming, "Barbeque." It was near lunchtime, so I whipped a U-turn at the next interchange and returned to the shack. There were inner tubes lying around the perimeter of the building, which signaled that I had arrived at either a put-in or take-out for river tubers. I exited the Mustang, and approached a middle-aged man who appeared to be local, and inquired as to the quality of the food. His response was, "Best barbeque between Kansas City and the Atlantic Ocean!" I had not sampled barbeque within that geographic description, but I decided to try it anyway.

I ordered a wood-smoked beef brisket sandwich with no sauce, and I was pleasantly surprised at the size and delightful aroma coming from my fare. Upon sampling it, I discovered that I had stumbled on a culinary gem. The flavor of the beef was something I had never experienced. The combination of the smoke and the seasoned rub was exquisite: not overly salty, and without heavy spices that overwhelmed the taste of the smoked meat. I tried to drag the recipe for the dry rub from any employee who would speak with me, but it was a fruitless effort. It was a family confidence, not to be sold, bartered, or revealed for fear of terminal reprisal. The meat was tender and moist, and I became a fan of beef brisket to the point that it is about all I will order when visiting a barbeque joint to this day.

Reluctantly, I left the little shack on the river and continued my journey along I-40, which passes just a couple of miles north and east of the Great Smoky Mountains National Park, through the Appalachians. These beautiful mountains are much different than the Rockies, which are more jagged and are in a less humid climate. But the Appalachians have a lushness that is missing in the west. The various shades of green created by the diversity of the trees are mesmerizing as they stretch over the rolling mountains in vast panoramas that are unlike anything I had observed before.

Somewhere near the Tennessee–North Carolina border, I was following a pickup truck pulling a flatbed trailer loaded with several steel pipes, which were about four inches in diameter and maybe eight feet long. I normally follow at a safe distance, and this was no exception. I was traveling at a speed of about seventy miles per hour when one of the pipes slid from the trailer, hit the pavement, and rolled beneath the front tires perpendicular to the path of my Mustang. It happened so fast that I had no time to brake. It felt like I had hit a brick wall. There was moderate traffic around me on the multiple lane highway, and my first thought was that this would blow out one or two of my tires and be the beginning of a multicar pileup. With a deafening bang, the car took slightly to the air as the front tires rolled over the pipe, and the same thing happened as it progressed to the rear. When the pipe was behind me, I was surprised to see that I was still in my lane and moving forward, and I needed only a slight correction to remain under control.

I braked to slow the vehicle, and in the rearview mirror, I was gratified to see that every automobile behind me was operated by a driver who skillfully missed the projectile; there were no accidents as a result. I pulled over because by the sound of that pipe hitting the Mustang, I was certain that it had torn half of the undercarriage from the car. After inspecting both the underside and the body of my Mustang, I guardedly determined it would be safe to proceed. I pulled cautiously into the right-hand lane and moved slowly, anticipating strange noises, vibrations, and shudders. To my relief, none of those occurred. We were moving smoothly with only normal engine, tire, and highway noise. In the next town harboring a Ford dealership, I had the car lifted and inspected, and I was assured that nothing appeared damaged. Yes, there are miracles.

With little more to alert my adrenaline the remainder of the day, I arrived in Charleston about four hours later, in the early evening. The hotel in the downtown district was small and very clean, and the staff was incredibly helpful. After unloading and moving my things to the room; I managed to dump my cooler off the luggage cart in the middle of the lobby. I returned to the registration desk to inquire of a nearby pub where I might extort a nice gin on the rocks and celebrate the end of this day. I was directed to a hotel across the street that boasted a popular rooftop bar.

Once there, I was delighted to find it to be congenial spot with a long bar, at which there were about three stools available. I squeezed myself into one not because the others and I convening there were too hefty, but because there were more stools than stool spaces at this bar. It was okay because I only had to keep my elbows tight to my side and lift the glass directly from the bar surface to my parched lips with a smooth lift, using only my elbow, to feel the silky Sapphire extraction of juniper berries glide over my tongue and drop into my belly, where it created a wonderful, tingly, burning sensation that left my adventures of the day behind me. The people were friendly, the place was crowded, and the people-watching was at its finest. I offered my stool to the female half of a middle-aged couple standing nearby, and they quickly engaged me in conversation. They were from a small town nearby and had come in for the day; this was one of their favorite places. Before the evening was over, I had been given full-scale insight on where to go and what to see. They had purchased a few drinks for me behind my back, and before they left, they invited me to visit them and stay as long as I liked. Had it not been for my prepaid lodging in Key West, I undoubtedly would have accepted that offer.

Thus began my stay in beautiful Charleston, South Carolina.

Chapter 22

All-American City

I had enjoyed a few drinks and a fine dinner the night before. Upon waking my first morning in Charleston, I decided that I needed a long walk to offset the potential for expansion of my already adequate waistline. I inquired about a waterfront walk and was directed to the Waterfront Park, which was a block from the hotel entrance. My four-mile journey began there and proceeded along the entire length of the park: past a large playground, the wharf, and the yacht club; along Battery Street; and ultimately to the end of Murray, Avenue where the US Coast Guard station is located. That ended the accessibility to the waterfront, so I returned the way I had come.

Along this route bordering Charleston Harbor were many historical reminders of the Civil War, in the form of cannons and other military placements. There was a view of the old Ft. Sumter, the spot where the first shot of the war was fired. Interestingly, I later learned that the first submarine attack in history occurred in the harbor. Ft. Sumter is now a national monument.

It was difficult not to notice that the people I passed on this walk were mostly younger, were professional looking, and appeared to be in rather good physical shape. There were very few obese people in this area, and there were many jogging or walking. I spent a good part of the balance of the day walking the downtown streets of Charleston.

During my stay in Charleston, I had several memorable experiences. The most memorable was the evening that I had finished dinner and chose to return to the rooftop bar. There I seated myself at a bar stool not far from a servers' work station. I ordered another gin and was people-watching when, to my delight, about a half-dozen smiling and laughing young ladies ranging from early twenties to early thirties entered through a door near where I was sitting.

They proceeded to approach the bar near me. A few took the available stools, and the others stood in a semicircle around the seated girls. They were a happy lot, and with their drinks in hand, they discussed the events of their day at work. Most comments were in the form of humorous ridicule of associates or clients, which were followed by giggling and laughing. They were all attractive and were wearing what appeared to be standard summer attire for professional women in downtown Charleston: above-the-knee skirts or dresses of rather light material, tan bare legs, and high-heel dress shoes. I thought I had died and entered the Promised Land. I had heard the term eye candy before. If it were listed in a dictionary, a picture of this group would be adjacent to the definition as a visual supplement.

Soon, I caught a glimpse of something strange moving toward the wait station. It was a rather slight man wearing a pink seersucker suit, with white belt and white shoes. Now, I had only observed something like this in old Vaudeville type movies or unbearable advertisements throughout my adult life. I guess I was staring while trying to figure out if this was standard summer attire for professional men in downtown Charleston, if there was some sort of live entertainment coming up later, or if there was a circus in town.

In any event, someone tapped me on the shoulder and said, "Can't take your eyes off of that, can you?" I turned, and one of those young women next to me was standing so close that I could feel her breath in my ear.

"Actually, I was just trying to figure it out," I replied.

"Well, don't. He comes in here often, as we do, and he always dresses that way. To our knowledge, he does not do it for professional reasons, and he is always alone with neither female nor male companionship. He does display some femininity when he speaks."

We bantered a bit more about this strangely dressed person, and for whatever reason, the girl invited me to join her and her friends.

We spent a bit less than an hour at that bar, where I learned all of their names and the nature of their careers. I hoped that I was not driveling or panting loudly, because I couldn't recall my having been surrounded by such beautiful young women in such numbers in my lifetime. They asked why I was there. I explained how I had lost Susie, the bizarre way in which my career had ended, and my deciding to take an extended road trip on the first day of my retirement.

Suddenly one of them announced, "Our table is ready." My heart sank. I did not want this night to end. It turned out the table was on the outside deck, directly in front of a young fellow who was singing very palatably, accompanied by his acoustic guitar. The girls, almost as one, informed me that they had reserved the table when they'd arrived, and they included a spot for me. My heart took a giant leap.

We sat at that table for probably three hours. These women talked of their friends, their associates, and themselves. However, they never once excluded me from their conversations. They often asked of my experiences as they related to theirs, and although most of the time the discussions were fueled by humor, they were wholesome. I have never in my life felt so comfortable with strangers, and these people were forty years my junior.

When I had decided that due to my relatively early tee time for golf the next day, it would behoove me to retire before closing time, I began thinking about the check. Embarrassingly, it did cross my mind that this might have been a set up to get a sugar daddy to pick up the tab at the end of the evening. I could not have erred more. When I got the attention of our server and requested my check, she paused and said, "Oh, no, sir. These ladies have paid your tab." I almost cried. When I rose from my chair, they all did the same, and one by one they gave me a firm hug before I left.

To me, Charleston, South Carolina, is the kindest, most beautiful city on earth. I will vividly remember that evening and those beautiful women until the day that I die.

I played golf in Charleston the following day. Afterward, I decided to check into one of the horse-drawn carriage tours of the local historical sites. I had noticed several of these rigs passing by during my walk on the previous day. Most of them were filled with one or more families, generally with one or two children who seemed to require more attention than they were receiving, and who had vocally dominated the airwaves for all around to enjoy. Not wanting to share in that type of close encounter, I opted for the private tour. Although much more expensive than the group tours, it was worth every dollar.

The coachman and tour guide was a jovial sort who somewhat reminded me of Santa Claus, yet he was not in that age group. He was probably about fifty. We toured for about an hour and a half, and from Ft. Sumter to the haunted mansions, I got an inspiring rendition of the history of the city and the Civil War, along with the people who left their legacies here. Not having to share my guide with others was a fortunate thing because I could inquire about anything that entered my mind, and I received an instant and comprehensive response. I believed everything that he threw at me, not knowing to what extent it may have been embellished. I do believe that he was very knowledgeable, but he was also a fantastic storyteller. What a great afternoon.

The following morning, I decided to take a long walk, heading the opposite direction of the waterfront stroll I had taken before. After a mile and a half, I came upon the Arthur Ravenel Jr. Bridge, which crosses over Town Creek and the Cooper River to Mt. Pleasant. The bridge appeared to be quite long, but I decided, "Oh, well," and headed across. I later learned that the bridge is about two and a half miles long. As I crossed the bridge, I noticed an aircraft carrier, a submarine, and what appeared to be a destroyer moored in a group below and to my right. This piqued my interest.

I left the bridge and wandered toward the vessels. Soon after, about another mile, I found myself at the entrance to the Patriots Point Naval and Maritime Museum. I paid the nominal fee and entered.

I have always had a curiosity about life on an aircraft carrier, so I approached this vessel first. I was standing before the USS *Yorktown*, a carrier first commissioned on April 15, 1943, when I was one year old. It served in World War II and the Vietnam War before being decommissioned in 1970. Although smaller than today's carriers, it seemed enormous to me. Once inside, I was able to see the planes on the various decks where they were stored, maintained, or repaired. Even these World War II planes were larger than I had imagined. I spent a good deal of time studying the vessel, its functions, and the planes it supported.

Upon reaching one deck, I was surprised to see a sixties vintage spacecraft there before me. It was apparently a replica of the Apollo 8 capsule that was recovered, along with the astronauts, by this carrier in December 1968.

I worked my way to the highest point on the ship, which is located on the island, a very narrow and high tower, on one side of the vessel. It houses the command for both the flight deck and the ship's operations. The access was a very narrow and steep staircase that sweltered in the heat of the day. It was difficult to maneuver in this cramped space, particularly with the many other folks attempting to negotiate it. I had spent a couple of hours on the carrier, and it was now time to move on to my next favorite warship, the submarine.

I was anxious to board the USS *Clamagore*, a World War II vintage submarine. If I thought it was difficult to maneuver in the tower of the aircraft carrier, I only had to wait a short time to appreciate its ample space compared to this submarine. The galley, bunks, heads, and all work areas were built for the seven dwarfs. I cannot imagine sailors having to live in such tight quarters for extended periods. Many of the people who were touring the craft at the same time turned back and exited quickly due to claustrophobia. Those of us who have never experienced combat duty can never fully appreciate what those brave people endured both in exposure to danger and in living conditions to assure our freedom.

I returned to my hotel by my original route and spent my last evening dining at a restaurant before retiring. The next day, I planned to head for Key West—Ernest Hemingway and Jimmy Buffet Land! If I were not financially committed to this next segment of my trip, I would probably have extended my stay in Charleston, because I had never been so impressed with any other city.

Chapter 23

Harbour Town

The next morning, I took my time packing, grabbing breakfast, and checking out. It was going to be a short travel day, and I did not want to be rushed leaving Charleston. In fact, I decided to walk along the waterfront out to the coast guard station, where I had been my first night in town. Upon my return, I said my farewell and reluctantly left Charleston.

My next stop was Hilton Head Island, South Carolina, home of the Harbour Town Golf Links, where the PGA stages what is now known as the RBC Heritage golf tournament. The course is famous not only for its skill requirements, but also for the picturesque lighthouse that greets one from the eighteenth tee box.

Although my golf outings were always enjoyable on this trip, as well as at other times, they were never a high point of an adventure. It is always difficult to get that little ball into that little hole with those sticks made of metal and other materials, which only a rocket scientist can explain or understand. It is sometimes so difficult that I often forget to stop and smell the roses along the way.

Golf clubs often claim bragging rights to the degree of difficulty over other courses, but when they actually succeed in being the hardest

known to man, I may play an entire round without knowing whether
I am in a tropical rain forest or in the middle of Death Valley. People
can often play a course for the first time and, following the round,
describe each shot made, the length from tee to green on each hole,
and what the surrounding scenery was as they navigated the course.
I can tell you at which hole I discontinued keeping score, how many
expletives I used on each hole, and how often my GPS indicated that
I had only advanced the ball half the distance intended for the club
with which I had launched it.

In any event, after the short drive from Charleston to Hilton Head,
I pinpointed the location of the golf course so that I could find
it quickly for my tee time the next morning. I spent some time
exploring the area, and then settled in for some drink and dinner
before retiring to the Holiday Inn Express.

The next morning, I prepared for a fairly early tee time, and after
packing and checking out, I made my way to Harbour Town, where
I found myself on the first tee in rather short order. I was paired
with three other players who were younger and significantly better
adapted to the game than I was.

I wisely played from the same tees as they. Although I wear my age
as it is, I feel about twenty years younger, and of course, I feel that
I can still do anything I could do those short twenty years ago. I
thought I could hit it out there with these young bucks. It was not
to be. I found myself feeling that I belonged on the geriatric tees. In
golf, whatever happens is where you are. No going back, no do-overs.

Well, I tried to make up my lack of distance by swinging harder,
which is a beginner mistake. I was on a famous golf course and was
not about to let it beat me. It did. The course demands precision.
When one swings harder, both accuracy and distance diminish.
I saw places at Harbour Town that most of the wildlife there was

unaware existed. It was a frustrating and embarrassing experience—until I reached the tee at hole seventeen.

This is where golf meets water. I don't remember specifically the view from the tee, but I have since dreamed of about 160 yards of salt grass, murky and brackish water, and many other plants unidentifiable to me stretching out toward a small flag, which was my target. My first shot made it about halfway. My second shot made it about three-fourths of the way. I was going to hit a third, but my playing partners decided it was time to move on and whisked me away.

Finally, I reached the eighteenth tee. There before me was the famous Harbour Town Lighthouse. I had watched a great deal of televised PGA golf over the years, and one of the most appealing sights was that red and white striped lighthouse beckoning from the end of that beautiful fairway. I began to weep and wished that Susie could have shared this moment. I don't remember playing that final 444 yards, and the trials of the other 17 holes were forgotten. I missed having my playing partner on this golfing adventure, and my heart was breaking.

Chapter 24

Opportunity

I stayed on the island another night and proceeded south the next morning. I have little recall of my trip through Georgia because I was focused on reaching Key West.

Once I entered Florida, I made a beeline for the coast and Highway A1A. I had visited Amelia Island before and wanted to pass that way again on this excursion. It was a perfect day, weather wise. I had the convertible top down and a Dean Martin album on the CD player. Off to my left, a pod of about one hundred pelicans was sailing just above the Mustang's level. They were traveling single file and at about the same speed as the car, and they seemed as if they were close enough to reach out and touch. The stretch of road I was on seemed devoid of traffic, although there were beach houses scattered between the road and the water. The pelicans traveled with me for about four or five miles. I had never seen anything quite like that before, nor have I to this day.

Once they broke the formation and headed out over the water, I continued on until I reached the ferry that crossed the St. Johns River to Ft. George Island. I pulled into the staging area and arrived just as the last vehicle pulled onto the ferry and the gate was closed. The parking attendant guided me to the spot where I would wait until the next ferry began loading. Although I would normally be rather fidgety while waiting, this was a welcomed break from driving, and it gave me an opportunity to check voice mail. I had not yet begun texting.

Soon, the ferry arrived and began unloading. Once the barriers were lifted and it was time for my group to load, I was motioned forward by the attendant and was the first car on. Upon boarding the ferry, a young girl about twenty and quite attractive waved me to the front and stopped me directly at the exit gate. I would be the first to disembark. The young lady continued loading the ferry until it more resembled an opened can of automobile-shaped sardines than a watercraft.

I was not paying close attention, but when the vessel was fully loaded and beginning to leave the dock, the little lass who had been directing the cars opened the passenger door of the Mustang and sat down. "I just love your car," she remarked. As I had done many times before, I thanked her and expressed how much I appreciated having the car, and how much I enjoyed it. She continued with small talk. "Where are you from? What brings you to Florida?" And then the shocker. "Where are you going?"

"Key West."

"Can I go with you?"

I was stunned. By now, one would guess that I had not been with a woman for a very long time. My mind was a Mix Master as I processed this request.

First came the positive thoughts as I scrutinized her attractive young face, her shapely figure, and those legs emerging from very short shorts.

Then I came to my senses and thought of the possibility that she might not be as honest as she looked. She might not be over sixteen or seventeen. She might have a mean father, jealous husband, or violent boyfriend.

Then I thought, *Boy, this trip is supposed to be an adventure. Why don't you see where this might take you?*

I asked her, "Are you serious?"

"Yes. I promise I won't be any trouble, and I can pay my own way."

We were getting close to the dock on Ft. George Island, and there was little time before I must make a decision.

Finally, I told her that I was flattered that she wanted to join me, but as I had previously explained to her, it had not been that long since I'd lost my wife of many years, and I needed to continue this journey alone. She said that she understood and was sorry that the timing was such, because she thought it would be fun for both of us. With that, she went back to directing traffic off the ferry.

This girl was at least forty years my junior and was very attractive— and I had just declined her offer to join me in Key West. What an ego boost that was! However, it was a good decision because I was in no mental shape to pursue what lay down that path.

I followed route A1A, which passes the entry to the TPC at Sawgrass in Ponte Vedra Beach. Once again, a chill came over me. Susie and I had played this legendary course while at a conference on Amelia Island. She had scored a birdie on one of the three pars, with a great tee shot and an even better putt. It was strange that after a year and a half of living alone in Pueblo and passing all of the places that held memories, I had never felt the loneliness and grief that I was experiencing as I traveled seventeen hundred miles from home.

I continued on in somewhat of a daze. The contradicting emotions of the day had drained me, and I felt a deep sadness as I checked into a room in one of the chain motels off the highway and facing the Intracoastal Waterway near Titusville. The hotel was old and appeared to be preparing for either complete renovation or demolition, and the nearby restaurant that I chose was about the same. In any event, I made it through the night with reasonable rest, and I woke the next morning in better spirits, anxious to proceed to the Keys.

Chapter 25

Overseas Highway and Paradise

I followed I-95 south past Ft. Lauderdale and then as far as it would take me into the Miami area, before it ended and dumped me into the middle of metro traffic. I escaped the area with minimal delay and was finally in light traffic, headed for Key Largo.

I had planned a bit of time in Key Largo because I had been told it was the resting place of the *African Queen*, the boat used by Humphrey Bogart and Katherine Hepburn in the movie of the same name. The boat is on display at the Holiday Inn on Key Largo, and it has been added to the National Register of Historic Places.

I went to observe the old watercraft, and it looked every bit as old as it was. There was a lot of rust and an overall unkempt look. The boat was built in 1912 for the British East Africa Railway and had operated productively until 1968. It had a steel hull and was powered with a coal-burning steam boiler. The movie was filmed in 1950, and the boat was moved to the United States in the seventies. Seeing the craft and learning of its history was interesting, but I would suggest seeing the movie before such a visit, because it would make the experience much more meaningful. (I did see the movie after the fact, and having seen the boat firsthand did add to the intrigue.)

My next stop was Islamorada, where at the World Wide Sportsman rests the replica of the *Pilar*, the boat owned by Ernest Hemingway. While I was touring the boat, someone mentioned that he had heard that Hemingway had taken this exact boat on a fishing expedition in the thirties and decided to purchase one just like it. This boat was beautiful, and I was envious. The beautiful wood, sleek design, and comfortable interior captivated me. The mystic of Hemingway and his lifestyle fascinated me, and I was heading right into one of the sites where his legend was born.

It was time to proceed to Key West. I was now about eighty miles from Mile Marker Zero on Highway 1 in Key West. To say the least, there are an incredible number of things to see and do in the Keys. Great bars, where one can become lost in thought or from reality. Great access to fishing, snorkeling, sunsets, crystal-clear seawater, and a whole new outlook on life. There are abundant fresh seafood eateries, whether a shack along the road or a swank restaurant. On the Keys, there was literally something for everyone. All of these things were calling me as I traveled the last few miles to the vertex of my somewhat orbital path from Pueblo and back again.

I could not be swayed, because Key West had become a legendary place to me. The historical significance, the stories told by my friends who had traveled there, the lore of Ernest Hemingway and, of course the lifestyle promoted by Jimmy Buffet drew me to this objective.

The trip along the Overseas Highway is something that everyone should experience at least once. The sights were unlike anything I had seen before. An unimaginable palate of colors are released from the clear waters as passing clouds and varying depths create a kaleidoscopic effect for the attentive traveler. Islands created by red mangroves sprouting from the sand and mud of the shallower waters dot the waterscape wherever one gazes. As I reached the final few miles proceeding into Key West, I felt disappointment that the trip was ending. The journey surely was every bit as exciting as I'd expected the destination to be.

I checked into my hotel on Duval Street. Thus began my few days on Key West.

There were many highlights in my visit to this city, however on my first night in town, I decided to simply walk around and observe. I was amazed but not surprised at the party atmosphere almost everywhere I ventured. It was early evening, and already many of the restaurants had waiting lines outside. Most of the taverns were crowded and quite noisy. Upon asking, I discovered that this was the first wave of families and older folks, and that the young people would surface much later, when it would become even wilder and crazier.

I recall sticking my head into several eating establishments, only to be told that I must wait for an hour or more. Finally I was able to locate one with a shorter wait time, and I succeeded in satiating my by then voracious appetite. Afterward, I found a relatively quiet lounge not far from the restaurant. Now, maybe I could have a couple of sapphires on the rocks and relax after what had turned out to be a rather long but very interesting day.

The Sapphire worked, and I headed back to the hotel for a good night's rest. It was comforting to know that I would not have to get behind the wheel of the Mustang the next day.

The following morning, following a hearty breakfast, I decided to walk the town. I started by heading south on Duval Street to the southernmost point in the continental United States. I continued until I reached South Street, which I followed to the famed buoy located where South Street intersects with Whitehead. The marker was surrounded by a rather large contingent of tourists, and although it is interesting to stop for a moment and reflect at being so far from the North Pole and so near to Cuba, I could not understand the fascination lasting for more than a few minutes. That's how much time I spent, and then I sauntered off to take a peek at the Hemingway House.

I am always intrigued at being in a spot where someone who had a major impact on something of global significance has lived. In this case, it was literary, but Hemingway also had intrigued me personally through his writing by reflecting a disheartened view of life, as evidenced by his suicidal demise, while living a lifestyle that appeared to me to be adventuresome and fulfilling.

The old home was the destination for a large crowd of tourists. I am not one who is comfortable mingling with such massive groups, and so I made a rather hasty jaunt through the dwelling. I had seen many old mansions throughout the years and gave little attention to the room size, décor, and architectural significance of the structure. I was more interested in the areas where the author had spent his time writing and relaxing. The atmosphere in which a person works and unwinds always intrigued me; that is one way that I get a feel for a person's character. I was satisfied that my perceptual analysis of Hemingway was validated by what I observed, because these areas were pretty much what I had expected. With that, I moved outside.

Within the boundaries of the yard surrounding the house, I noticed a number of cats lounging. I quickly located a person who could explain, and I was told that the felines were descended from a cat owned by the author and that the original cat was blessed with six toes rather than the ordinary five, or something like that. Apparently some of these cats were endowed with a like mutation.

The other notable thing outside was the swimming pool. I understood that it was built for a great deal of money, and that Hemingway was not pleased with the expenditure. A penny is lodged between flagstones on the patio, adjacent to the pool, evidently to symbolize the comment to his wife and the contractor: "You've spent all but my last penny. So you might as well have that." He did supposedly design the pool himself, and it must have been magnificent in its day. It was the only in-ground pool within a hundred miles at the time.

I moved on to wander around Key West doing one of my favorite things, which is observing people who live outside of a popular tourist area, trying to look and act the part of one of the local inhabitants. There are two categories of these people: Those who research before leaving home and bring their getup with them, and those who arrive and buy theirs from the local tourist traps. It's fun to watch them all try to fit in.

I grabbed lunch at a café and then continued walking around for a while before heading back to the hotel to rest for a bit. On my way to the room, I asked the concierge about something to do in the evening hours other than patronize a drinking establishment. He suggested a sunset cruise on one of the schooners in the nearby marina. I asked him to pick one for me and inquire about a reservation for that evening. Fortunately, there was one space available on one that, although a larger three-mast craft, limited the number of passengers to ensure a more intimate experience.

Sunset occurs in Key West between 8:00 and 8:30, so I boarded the vessel about 6:30 or 7:00. The schooner was magnificent; it had great teak decks, and was well maintained and clean. The crew was remarkable, and the wine and hors d'oeuvres were spectacular.

The passengers were primarily couples, however there were two or three family groups. One of the crewmembers asked how I'd chosen Key West. I briefly explained my loss of Susie, the events leading to my retirement, and my love for being on the road. He then served me some wine and snacks, after which I retreated to an unobtrusive area of the ship. I wanted to enjoy the experience lost in thought and not feeling an obligation to make conversation with someone.

Evidently, the crew member passed my tale onto others on deck, because I had a series of visitors come sit next to me and strike up the very conversations I had hoped to avoid. I was pleasant to all and was invariably invited to join each group that was represented. I respectfully declined those invitations, and after about a half hour, they finally got the drift. I was left to enjoy a magnificent sunset along with plenty of wine, cheese, and an assortment of other culinary delights.

Etched in my mind are the final few minutes of the sun's departure as a large, double-masted clipper sat on a direct line between the sun and our boat. As the sun dropped below the horizon, it seemed to magnify the boat, and with all of the background colors, it made a fitting end to nature's performance. It's one of the most remarkable sights I can remember.

Upon returning to the dock, I decided to visit one of the most talked-about places in Key West, at least among my friends and acquaintances that had visited this unusual resort: Jimmy Buffet's Cheeseburger in Paradise. I thought to myself, *Why not have one in such a fabled place?*

When I entered the establishment, I was greeted with a packed house creating more abrasive clamor than I have ever experienced. I saw a small empty table and proceeded to sit, where I was immediately approached by a less-than-personable employee who informed me that I was not to sit there. For what reason, I was not told. I stood and waited for about twenty minutes to be seated, and I was never spoken to again. Other people entered and were seated almost immediately, and I made eye contact with several employees but apparently did not fit the mold to be a patron of this legendary spot. I finally gave up and retreated to another location, where I was immediately seated and enjoyed a fine cheeseburger and a few attitude-adjusting beers. The most popular joint is not necessarily the most enjoyable joint!

Previously, I had made arrangements through the hotel concierge to meet a bone fishing guide early the next morning. I followed instructions and arrived at the dock at about sunrise thirty. The guide had planned the exact trip I had hoped for. It was a half day fishing flats about forty minutes from the dock. I had many fly fishing buddies from the old days in Aspen, and many had talked of their bone fishing experiences. This was kind of on my bucket list.

The guide made certain that he understood exactly what I had in mind and checked to make sure that I was comfortable with the equipment that he had available. Then we were off across the crystal-clear tropical waters to the storied flats. The trip took about forty-five minutes, and the clear, rather shallow water revealed an abundance of plant life, along with an occasional large sea going creature. It was invigorating.

We arrived at the flats that the guide had chosen, and I felt as though I had been planted in the middle of one of the documentaries I had watched about such fishing. The shallow, wadeable water was relatively free of vegetation and was as clear as a glass of highly filtered vodka. Once shown, I was able to detect the direction of the currents crossing the flats, and the hunt for the skittish bonefish began.

I hadn't fished for some time, and I required a short bit of tutoring on my casting techniques for this type of fishing before we began. It took several practice casts, but it soon came back to me, and I became quite comfortable with the legendary double haul, which is a method of casting that greatly increases the distance one can attain with a fly line.

According to the guide, there were few if any bonefish occupying the flat at this time. I had no idea what I was looking for, but suddenly he directed my attention directly ahead of me, about seventy-five feet away. There I spotted a shadow moving almost directly at the boat. I gave one short practice cast and then let fly with my newly reacquired double haul. The line dropped quietly on the water, and the fly rolled out from that point and dropped exactly on the target the guide had suggested. I listened intently as he encouraged me with the retrieving technique. The bonefish was attracted to the fly and was gaining on it rapidly! The guide did everything in his power to keep me calm as the fish approached nearer and nearer. The whole scene was getting very close to the boat, and the guide directed me to calmly lift the tip of the rod. I hadn't fished in years, this was a bucket list adventure, and I was about to hook a bonefish! I half jerked the tip of the rod about two feet into the air, and the fly made a rather unnatural move. The bonefish disappeared, as did my adrenaline rush.

"I said calmly," he muttered. I apologized, to which he smiled and said, "It almost always happens with the first one." My heart was fractured a little, but at last I had seen one of the elusive fish and had persuaded it to look at my fly.

On our return trip to the dock, we ran across a school of tarpon, another sought-after sporting fish found in these waters. The guide set us up to intercept them, and soon I was in a like situation as I had found myself in with the bonefish. This time, the fish looked to be three or four feet long, and if caught, it would be by far the largest thing I had ever dreamed of catching on a fly rod. The bonefish was probably about twenty to twenty-four inches long.

This time, the adrenaline rush was magnified by the same ratio as the difference in the sizes of the two fish, and as the tarpon approached the boat, I made the same childish mistake I had made before. The magnificent fish disappeared. Thus ended my fishing experience out of Key West.

I tipped the guide and, upon his recommendation, sat at one of the restaurants right there on the dock. I had a nice lunch of something, and conch fritters. Those fritters were great!

After lunch, I decided to walk around the town a bit because it was my last day there. I came upon a cruise ship terminal with one of the monster vessels just leaving the dock. It was astonishing that on every side of that ship was either a navy or coast guard Zodiac, a small, inflatable craft used to patrol local coastal waters. These Zodiacs had what appeared to be about 50-caliber machine guns mounted on the forward deck and manned by a gunner. I was never able to ascertain why they were escorting this ship, but they followed it until it was in open water.

Chapter 26

Alligators and Good Friends

My last night in Key West was rather uneventful. I was, after all, in no mood to join the boisterous crowds, and I was not looking to meet a new friend. I had a quiet dinner and headed to bed.

The next day, I headed to Naples on the west coast of Florida to visit my friends of many years, Frank and Vicki Scott. The Scotts were bank customers back in my Breckenridge days, and Susie and I had played a lot of tennis with them as well as enjoyed many an evening in one of Breckenridge's more notable night spots.

I rose early because today's trip would take me back through the Miami area to near Ft. Lauderdale, where I would head west on I-75 toward Naples. The trip back up Highway 1 was beautiful but otherwise uneventful, other than that discouraged feeling one gets when leaving a place that has such history and charm, knowing it may be the only visit.

I made it through the Miami traffic with few aggravations and was soon on my way across I-75, Florida's "Alligator Alley." There is a reason it's tagged that way. As one travels this stretch of road across the Everglades, on both sides of the freeway are what I assume are drainage canals that are visible for the entire stretch of road until just outside of Naples. When traveling this route, I try to observe the wildlife on the portion bordering my side of the road. Something that makes time more fleeting is to count the alligators observed in the canal. This trip was one of the most productive I can remember. I counted just over 100 alligators on this 109-mile corridor. That's about one alligator every mile. Wow!

I arrived at the Scotts' charming home, which was situated on a man-made lagoon in one of the picturesque neighborhoods of Naples. The kitchen and dining areas directly overlooked the lagoon, and the living area overlooked the deck and the inviting pool, which were enclosed with heavy screening to keep the pests outside. The floor-to-ceiling windows in the abundant living area folded away to merge the deck and pool into the indoor space. Of the many times I had visited them, only once did I fail to see porpoise frolicking in that lagoon.

Frank and Vicki were the ultimate hosts. Whether I wanted to try my hand at photographing pelicans, play golf, attempt my hand at tennis, or go sightseeing, they fit my wishes into their schedules. First thing each morning, I was greeted with bacon frying along with fresh ground coffee, fruit, and eggs to order.

They went so far as to find me a tennis partner, which allowed me to join them for their weekly mixed double round robin, followed by cocktails and maybe a burger. This newfound partner was a much better player than I but seemed willing to tolerate my rather unorthodox approach to the game. I was not without some successes at tennis, but normally I was considered more a court jester than a serious student of the game.

On a later trip to visit the Scotts, this young lady tennis partner would be my first attempt at a formal date since my becoming single. As a gesture to thank her for enduring the embarrassment of being seen on the court with me, and to Vicki and Frank for their hospitality, I invited them out to dinner at a slightly upscale seafood restaurant near one of the marinas. The food was superb, the drink was even better, and the conversation was difficult to come by. I could not seem to find any words that made me comfortable—or worse, that I thought would make her comfortable. In any event, that part of the evening was a total bust, and that would be my last "date" for many months.

After a few days with my friends, it was time to say goodbye and begin the next leg of this adventure.

I left fairly early the next day and drove north on I-75 toward Tampa. Rather than hug the Gulf Coast on the peninsula, I chose to remain on the freeway to Tallahassee and then drop down to the coast as I approached the Florida panhandle. It seemed that I would get a better feeling for the Deep South that way, and I would avoid some of the congestion in the Tampa–St. Petersburg complex.

I spent the night in the Tallahassee area, and the next morning I headed toward Baton Rouge, a drive of about 450 miles. I headed south on US Highway 319 to connect with US Highway 98, which would take me along the Gulf Coast near Pensacola, where I would connect with I-10 into Alabama.

Generally, while traveling I try to get at least three miles of walking in, either before I leave or somewhere along the way. This day was no exception, and less than an hour after I arrived on the coastal highway, I noticed a rather eye-catching bridge crossing over to what appeared to be an island. My curiosity took control, the Mustang negotiated a sharp left turn, and over the bridge we went. I located a parking area and soon found myself walking on an uncluttered beach that stretched as far as I could see.

There were a couple of other automobiles in the parking lot, but for about an hour I saw not one other person on the beach. One thing I did see was what seemed to be a never-ending colony of crabs ranging in size from about a half dollar to the size of a coffee mug. They were scampering everywhere and often peeking out of holes they had burrowed into the sand. I had never seen anything like it.

I must have walked about three miles when I decided that if I wanted to make Baton Rouge that night, I should return to the car and be on my way. On the entire stretch of beach, I had seen two young men surf casting, and one middle-aged woman walking a small dog. There had not been another person in sight. This had been the most exhilarating walk I had taken on the entire trip, and it is etched in my mind forever. Maybe it's because of the crabs, or maybe the expanse of it all combined with the solitude. It was beautiful.

The balance of the day was an enjoyable road trip that showed me the best of the Deep South and the Gulf Coast. There was a mystical moss hanging from the trees that often formed a tunnel of greenery over the roadway. I stopped at one of the many roadside mom-and-pop gas stations and general stores along the way. I filled my trusty Mustang with fuel, and when I went to settle, I was informed that they did not accept credit cards, only cash or local checks. Fortunately, I carried a reasonable amount of cash for such occasions, but I was somewhat taken back with that comment in the twenty-first century.

The shoreline was generally beautiful where visible from the road, however the residential areas were apparently void of upscale neighborhoods. It was obvious that many areas suffered from poverty and had not changed in many decades. It was notable that whenever I stopped for fuel or a bite to eat, the local people seemed to be happy and contented. I think sometimes we define fortune in many different ways.

115

I continued toward Baton Rouge. I had decided to avoid New Orleans because the city was still reeling from the effects of Hurricane Katrina the year before. They certainly didn't need another curious tourist interfering with their rebuilding efforts. Somewhere near Baton Rouge, I found a motel near the freeway with one room available. I snatched it up. I inquired about a steakhouse nearby, and luckily the motel clerk suggested one next door to the property, referring to it as the best steak in the state.

I accepted his guidance and, after checking in, proceeded directly to it. I recall that it was a very good steak, but not necessarily exceptional. I was extremely hungry, and that undoubtedly contributed to my recollection of the quality. It had been a long day, and I was weary, but afterward, against my better judgment I strolled into the bar area of the restaurant for an after-dinner concoction.

The place was in the middle of a karaoke session, and because the performer on stage was a rather attractive young female, I decided to order a nice scotch and stay. The scotch arrived, and shortly thereafter, the young lady exited the stage. Just my luck. After a few minutes, during which the crowd became very loud in conversation, the room stilled momentarily and then erupted in loud applause. I could not imagine what could possibly cause such an uproar in a karaoke bar.

I soon found out. A slightly overweight person made his way through the crowd and stepped onto the stage. This individual resembled a cross between a 1970s hippie and a character from *Duck Dynasty*. He displayed a full head of matted hair that tumbled down over his shoulders, where it lay like greased burlap. His full facial hair also revealed what appeared to be a few months of neglect.

My thoughts were, "Wow! What have I done?" I guess I expected some local folksy thing or maybe ear-splitting acid rock, neither of which appealed to me. Whatever those thoughts were, they quickly abated, and I relearned not to judge a book by its cover.

The introductory music began, and the performer grabbed the microphone. When he sang, if one closed one's eyes, one would think he were in Las Vegas listening to Frank Sinatra. I have heard many singers try to emulate Sinatra both before and since, but none could rival his talent. I stayed until he left the stage, which was quite late, because he had an extensive repertoire.

This was another of the many experiences on this trip that brought tears to my eyes as I wished that Susie could have been there with me.

Chapter 27

Familiar Territory

I slept well for what remained of the night. The next morning, I would leave for Austin, Texas. I'd have a few days that would follow me for the rest of my life.

I traveled on I-10 into Houston, where I connected with US Highway 290 west into Austin. It was a rather uneventful travel day with the exception of the usual pockets of congestion in the Houston metro area. The trip was around 450 miles, and with some slowdown in Houston and an occasional rest break, it took about eight hours.

I arrived in Austin at about four in the afternoon and checked in to the Hilton Garden Inn near John Harris's home. The first evening there, John; his son Chris; Chris's fiancé, Tori; and John's daughter, Kelly, welcomed me to town by heading to dinner at their favorite nearby restaurant, Eddie V's Prime Seafood. We had always eaten well and drank plenty when we were together, and this evening was no exception.

Throughout this trip, I had looked forward to this stop in Austin. Although I had visited many times since leaving about twelve years before, it was always with a structured schedule; my time available was dictated by my responsibilities to the bank and to the holding company. Now, I was able to enjoy my visit to one of my favorite cities with no restrictions.

At the time Susie and I had left Austin, I had felt strongly that it was the best economic move for us. Leaving the city created a void that was never filled in Pueblo. The abundance of green foliage, Spanish moss hanging from the large live oak trees, and walking along the slow-moving Colorado River, which created the atmosphere of the Deep South; the friendly folks; the many picturesque and challenging golf courses; the Cajun food with availability of boiled crawfish; the barbeque restaurants; the cultural opportunities; the history; and the enthusiasm of a vibrant university town were a few of the things that I had missed while in Colorado.

Pueblo was a pleasant place, and I had many fond memories. There were also many close friendships that will last a lifetime. However, there were things about the community that, although not unusual for a city of its size, did not suit my way of life. Part of that stems from my wanderlust. I had experienced about eight career changes in seven locations over a period of about thirty years. I embraced change. Most of the people with whom I had business relationships in Pueblo had left town only long enough to obtain a college education, and then they returned to a comfortable environment surrounded by grade school and high school friends with whom they would spend the rest of their lives. I had lived in many cities in three states, and I had developed friendships in each. I had an entirely different philosophy toward life.

Now, being back in this city gave me a feeling of being home. I'd never felt that way in Pueblo. I suddenly had thoughts that this was where I wanted to spend my retirement years.

John, a mutual friend Tony, Chris, and I played golf over the many days of my stay. Whenever I came to town, golf had become somewhat of a ritual. John and I generally played at least one round at Pine Forest Golf Club in Bastrop, the course on which I'd once lived, and another round at Horseshoe Bay, a club situated on Lake LBJ about fifty miles from Austin.

After dinner, the youngsters headed out for the evening, and John suggested that we go check out one of the gentlemen's clubs not too far away. I had had a couple of alcoholic beverages, and my decision-making acumen had mostly departed for the evening, so I agreed.

We arrived at the club, The Yellow Rose, which had moderate traffic at the time. We chose a table at an elevated level, which provided a choice view of the main stage and the two or three, smaller, auxiliary, platforms where these beauties were performing. My seat was against the brass pipe railing at the back edge of this elevated area. This was good because I was not bothered by people, mostly scantily clad young bodies with faces that looked lovely in this dim light but that would probably make a freight train take a dirt road by the light of day, trying to squeeze between me and the chairs at an adjoining table.

We ordered a drink, which probably cost fifteen bucks even though it was just a house Chardonnay and was a somewhat meager pour. After relaying my adventures on the road for the day, John excused himself and walked away—I assumed to use the restroom.

John returned after a bit, and although he was conversant, something had changed. It was as if something was distracting him. I was facing him and making some kind of statement when someone whirled me around in the swivel chair on which I had been relaxing. I was face-to-face with, I guess, a woman whose face resembled a bulldog, as did her thick, squatty body. She barked, "I'm here to give you a lap dance."

I whined meekly, "Not right now, thank you."

She growled, "You don't have a choice—it's already paid for." With that, she began an exceptionally uncoordinated motion that I believe she thought was a dance, but that quickly became a physically abusive attack on my body. I tried to fight her off, but she was too strong. When I tried to speak, she grabbed me by the hair, slammed the back of my head against the brass rail, and (I believe while foaming at the mouth) shouted, "Shut up and pay attention!" My head throbbed. I was sure I could feel blood running down the back of my neck, and yet the worst had not occurred.

John sat there laughing loudly while enjoying his tasteless drink. Presently, this female hobbit began shedding her less-than-alluring clothing from her sweating torso. I had thought she had a dreadful face, but I hadn't yet observed her breasts, which were swinging like a pair of pendulums before my now terrified face. These were the most disgusting human body parts that one could imagine. They looked like two half-filled water balloons, and I was dreadfully concerned that something might burst one or both of them. I was lying back in the chair, and she was on top of me, trying to hump away. I attempted to slide out from under her and off the chair, but she thwarted my escape by slamming a knee into my groin. I now had ghastly pain in two places. She thrust her face up close to mine, and behold, there was a mustache! To avoid any contact, I turned my head to the side. Yikes! I could now observe the thick, muscular, hairy arm with scaly skin, and with which "she" supported herself over me while inflicting more agony. I was deathly afraid that she would put a foot up on the chair, and I would have to view the long hair protruding from there.

As quickly as it began, she shouted, "Time's up!" grabbed her sweat-stained garments, and disappeared. John had tears streaming down his face.

I remember nothing else the rest of that evening. The images are indelibly etched in a back corner of my mind, where they emerge on any occasion when I pass a gentleman's club, see a billboard advertising a gentleman's club, or (God forbid) consider joining a friend at a gentleman's club.

My welcome back was not over. John and his squad of progeny partiers had plans that included me for the next evening. He innocently asked if I would like to join them for an evening of music on Austin's famed East Sixth Street. I had been there several times before while living there, but not to catch a specific show following dinner at one of the many great restaurants. I foolishly agreed.

At that time, I lived a life of early to bed, early to rise. John and his offspring apparently didn't go by any timepiece unless they were in work mode. I don't recall where we had dinner that evening, but we didn't hit the pavement on Sixth until about 9:30 or 10:00 p.m., when I was usually in bed.

Chris, Tori, and Kelly were well-known in all of the bars through whose doors we passed. There were many, and each had either a specialty cocktail with both a substantial variety and substantial volume of spirits, or a bevy of young beauties walking the floor with a bandolier's belt of shot glasses and a pistol belt below with a bottle of tequila in the holster. I never pulled my wallet from my pocket, and I never had an empty glass. The streets were crowded with young people, and we entered wherever there was a different band playing music that seemed loud and caustic to my sixty-four-year-old ears, but which became more tolerable with each swallow of the devil's elixir.

My hosts were known to each bartender in every establishment. The drinks, most of which were complimentary, flowed freely. I believe that I might have been seen on the dance floor a time or two. I do distinctly remember that I was challenged to step up onto the small, round, elevated platform known as the VIP table at one of the saloons. I am not a dancer and will do almost anything to avoid becoming a spectacle in this arena. This night was going to be different. I accepted the challenge and invited Tori to join me. I danced to a standing crowd. I relished the hoots and what I took as applause. I hogged that pedestal for what seemed like an hour, but it was probably only a few minutes. I thought I replicated the moves of Travolta or Baryshnikov, but I am sure my moves would have made Ellen DeGeneres and Brad Garrett look like Fred Astaire and Ginger Rogers. I have not been contacted by *Dancing with the Stars*. Ten years later, I am told by the Harris clan that people on Sixth Street still ask about me!

I remember that as we left the last bar, the streets, which were previously crowded, were now devoid of humanity. I also know that I woke up the next morning in my hotel room, however I was not sure how I got there. My Mustang was in the parking lot, which was not good news, except that it appeared to be undamaged.

My hosts and I played golf a couple of times during this stop, but I don't recall any of it the day after my starring role on Sixth Street. Knowing John, he would have insisted on playing no matter the throbbing head and queasy stomach, and I would have gone along for the ride.

On a brighter note, I remained enthralled with the idea of moving back to Austin, and while there, I began to look at different areas that might appeal to me.

Chapter 28

Winds of Change

I left Austin after a few days, and the eight-hundred-mile trek from there to Pueblo is mostly west Texas, and eastern New Mexico. There are a lot of miles through rather desolate, sparsely populated terrain, and I found little to write about on this leg of my trip, although there are a number of historic and geographic points of interest along the way.

I was back in Pueblo and had a responsibility to both the liquidating trust of the bank holding company and to a developer whom I had known for many years who had asked me to provide advice on marketing and some financial issues. It was July, and over the next four months, I concentrated on working through these two projects.

I played golf with an afternoon golf league, created and sponsored by one of the large construction companies that had been a former customer of the bank. I looked forward to it weekly and enjoyed the time on the golf course with men from various professional backgrounds, because it kept me involved and informed about what was transpiring in the community. It was rather heart wrenching when it came time to leave after a couple of beers and a good deal of banter over the bets of the day, as well as the good or bad shots made. The sad part was when everyone left, talking about needing to get home to dinner, and I knew I would be returning to an empty house. It frequently hurt deeply, and these were the times when I missed Susie the most and when tears came somewhat freely, as I left the parking lot and returned home.

Stan Herman and I took a trip to Carlsbad Caverns in southern New Mexico, he on his motorcycle and me in my Mustang. We also took a trip to some little town south of Salina, Kansas, population about fifteen, to eat barbeque at an old, refitted high school. It was one of the most unusual trips I have taken. The place was literally in the middle of nowhere and was open only on Friday and Saturday. Parking was scarce, and the joint was packed.

Those things were a diversion from all of the humdrum of my two new responsibilities, neither of which I could get excited about because I knew that they were temporary and short-lived.

All of this time, I had Austin on my mind. The thought of leaving Pueblo became more prevalent because although winter in Pueblo had a number of warm, pleasant days, it was generally brown, windy, and cold. I finally decided to head to Texas and research possible housing options.

I called Jim Gibbons and got contact information for Tom, a friend of his who was a realtor, and whom I had met previously. I provided him with areas that I preferred, along with size, price range, and features that were important to me.

To purchase something in Austin, it was necessary that I procure a bridge loan on my residence in Pueblo, which was clear of debt. I contacted Anthony Andenucio, who had been a senior lender at the bank in Pueblo during my tenure there but had relocated to another bank nearby. He was able to accommodate me, the value was very adequate, and the repayment would be short term because I would sell my Pueblo home to repay it, and the market was strong.

I scheduled a trip to Austin, hopped into the minivan, and headed out. I took the van because traveling in the Southwest in winter can be icy and dangerous, and the van had front-wheel drive, whereas the Mustang had rear-wheel drive. The weight of the engine over the front wheels provided the van with much better traction for the conditions.

Soon I was in Austin, traveling from site to site with Tom and educating him on what I preferred and what was unacceptable. Although we did not find anything that would seem to work for me, it gave him ammunition with which to locate the perfect home for me. I returned to Pueblo to wrap up things over the next couple of months, and to prepare for the move.

I was probably the most dispensable person involved with the real estate development firm, and with a dwindling market in the area, cash flow did not warrant my continuing with them. I did help out on a pro bono basis when I could.

On the other hand, the most pressing and important thing that required my time was the liquidation of the trust prior to year's end. I spent the next several weeks concentrating on that issue and seeing it through.

My friend Jim Gibbons had met a woman who owned a townhouse in the same complex as his in the Aspen area, and they had become somewhat of an item. I had visited Jim a few times while this relationship was developing, and I was introduced to Gayle when the three of us had lunch together. Gayle was a very pleasant person who had a sense of humor that fit Jim perfectly. I was happy that Jim had found someone with which to share his time. He had grown children with families of their own, and he visited them somewhat frequently, but he seemed to have a desire for companionship that I had not yet acquired and probably never would.

At some time during these couple of months, during which I was hell-bent on transition, I received a call from Gayle. Her father, who had a home in Rancho Mirage, California outside of Palm Springs, was having his eightieth birthday on February 4, and her entire family would be attending. Jim was going to join them, but none of her family played golf, and he was going to be stuck there for several days with no one to golf with. She invited me to join them.

For the past few decades, I had heard many stories of the wonders of Palm Springs from many of my banking peers. I had joined them on golfing excursions to other out-of-state areas, but I had never been to Palm Springs. The city's history, its notoriety as a golfing mecca, and its reputation as a dining and party destination were appealing to me at this point in my life. I quickly accepted.

About two weeks later, a longtime friend of mine, John Wilkinson, called. John and I had met about forty-five years before, when we both were experiencing our first banking jobs as flunkies at the Colorado National Bank in Denver. We had become very close friends and had spent a great deal of time together hunting, fishing, skiing, and golfing. We were also known to occasionally have a beer while pursuing the opposite sex. I had moved to Denver from Alliance, Nebraska, at seventeen, and I guess I dressed the part. One day after lunch, John said, "Rather than return to work right now, we are going to make a stop."

I replied, "No, I have a lot on my plate, and I must get back."

John didn't accept the no, and he hustled me to Homer Reeds, a men's clothing store not far from the bank. John turned me over to a clerk he seemed to know well, and soon they had replaced my heavy wool sport coat (the only one I owned) with a blue blazer and gray slacks. They added a suit, shirts, ties, shoes and even socks. I could ill afford all of these items, but I discovered later that it was one of the best investments that I could have made. It was a day of transformation for me that shaped my life and my career.

John and I even purchased a boat together, which we used for fishing and some water-skiing. I was not handy in the water and had tried water-skiing only once. When John accelerated the boat to get me up on the skis, the tips went down rather than up. I suddenly found myself about twelve feet underwater, traveling somewhere around twenty miles an hour before finally releasing the tow rope and allowing myself to return to the surface. I never attempted that feat again.

This friendship waned somewhat when John fell in love and got married long before I did. We maintained contact over the years, and upon my moving back to Pueblo, close to the Denver area, we occasionally played golf and renewed our friendship.

The reason for John's call was that he and three other friends had scheduled a trip to Palm Springs to golf for four days. One of the friends had an emergency and was unable to join them. He was inviting me to fill the slot.

I asked what the dates were, and uncannily, it was the four days immediately preceding the days I had agreed to meet Jim. Once again, I accepted quickly. I had never been to Palm Springs, and now I was looking forward to a ten-day golfing marathon.

Chapter 29

Unique Christmas

The winter was windy and cold, we received more snow than usual, and I quickly tired of it all.

Christmas came rather abruptly. I had given the holidays little thought, and a few days before, I decided to spend Christmas Eve in Denver. I booked a room at a Marriott in a suburb on the south side of the Denver metropolitan area, which was near a McCormick and Schmick's Restaurant, where I made a reservation for Christmas Eve dinner.

On Christmas Eve day, sometime before lunch, I set the Mustang on a course due north on I-25. As I passed through Colorado Springs, I suddenly developed an urge for a cheeseburger. I was not familiar with places in the Springs where I could have a sit-down burger in a decent atmosphere. I kept my eyes peeled as I progressed north through the city. Nothing surfaced. Then as luck would have it, I spotted a Hooters sign on the left side of the interstate up ahead. I was in the far left lane of the three lanes of traffic, and I instinctively jerked my trusty steed to the far right just in time to enter the proper exit. Luckily, there was little traffic on this pre-holiday day.

I pulled into the parking area of the restaurant, and although there were no vehicles in the lot, I decided to walk to the entrance to see if it was open. Sure enough, it was. Now, Hooters has quite the atmosphere even when it is busy, with those young, scantily attired women charging around and serving the hordes who are drinking beer and consuming wings, burgers, and fries. It is quite another effect when one is the only patron in the place and the number of employees is not diminished.

I was greeted by more than one of the girls and had my pick of tables. I chose a high-top that overlooked the entire area. My assigned server approached, sat at the table (which is customary at Hooters), and provided me with a menu. After serving my iced tea, taking my order, and turning it in, she returned and sat again to visit.

She asked what I was doing out alone on this particular day. I responded with my story about losing my wife, selling the banks, and the incredible change in my life in a very short period. After wiping a tear, she retreated to return with the tall, juicy burger that I had ordered and was now able to contemplate.

I was left alone for a bite or two, and then she returned. We talked for a moment, and then as if by design, one of her buxom coworkers arrived and sat at the table. One by one, this continued until about eight of these twenty-something beauties were surrounding me. I asked about their schools, their jobs, their holidays, and anything else that I could think of to keep them interested. I wanted this lunch to never end.

They asked me many questions not only regarding my current situation but also regarding my past and my thoughts on current events. I felt like one of them, more so than a sixty-five-year-old should allow to happen.

Finally, it was time to go. I paid my tab with a much more than adequate tip and stood to leave. One by one, each of these delightful young women gave me a hug—and not just a little squeeze, but a hug that got all of my attention. There were many "Merry Christmases," and I turned away. This time the tear was wiped from my eye.

I gathered myself together, went to the car, and returned to the interstate. Soon I was approaching the metro area. It dawned on me that today, the Denver Broncos were scheduled to play. It was time to find a sports bar where I could watch the game and down a couple of brews.

Once again, I was unfamiliar with this type of establishment in the area, and I kept a lookout as I moved north. I did exit a couple of times, but the chosen establishments were closed. I finally exited northbound on Colorado Boulevard, a primary north-south artery in Denver. I passed many establishments that appeared to be what I was looking for, but all were idle for the holiday weekend.

Then a lit sign caught my eye: Shotgun Willie's. The Mustang whinnied and the tires squealed as I took a hard turn into the parking lot. Suddenly a vision flashed before my eyes: the hobbit at the Yellow Rose in Austin! I was approaching a gentleman's club! I was tired of driving and even more tired of searching. I had to work through this. Once again, there were only one or two vehicles in the parking lot. I hoped desperately that they were open and had a ton of large TVs available.

I entered, and my eyes took some time to adjust to the dark interior. I had never seen one of these places virtually devoid of customers, with only an occasional dancer on stage and with the balance of the entertainment staff lounging in chairs and watching football. The bright flash of light when I opened the door, caught everyone's attention, and one of the lovelies approached me, asking immediately if I would like a lap dance. I replied that I had come in to watch the game because I could find nothing else open. I also let her know that I just wanted to sit, have a beer, and wait for the game to start. I informed her that I had driven from Pueblo. She seemed very understanding.

Soon I was seated at a large table with an outstanding view of the TV set, and I had about a thirty-two-ounce draft of Heineken in my hand. The game was just beginning. At the first commercial break, the young lady who'd first approached me sidled up to the table and asked if she could join me, because that table was the best for viewing the game. I gladly agreed. After all, she was quite attractive, and so far she was much more personable than my previous experience in Austin. She sat and asked the same questions I had heard just a couple of hours before in Hooters. My responses were very much the same.

My beer was nearing empty, and she asked to refill it. I agreed. She returned with the next tall, frosty, foam-headed delicacy. She also returned with one of her cohorts, then another and another, until finally long-legged, very scantily dressed young females surrounded me. *What's with this day?* I thought.

The conversation continued much like the one before, and suddenly it was halftime. My little hostess took my hand, and pulled me to my feet. I was led to a very private little corner, and she proceeded to remove her top and give me the lap dance of my life. Nothing that was beyond what is allowed, but a lot of it. When she was finished, although she never asked, I handed her a wad of bills. She at first refused, but after convincing her it was Christmas and I had no one else to spend the money on, she accepted.

The ball game continued, and the girls came and went as they were called to the stage. I was surprised to find that the conversation was not of clothes, men, and all of the material things one would expect among those who had chosen this profession. After all, according to those surrounding me, there was a high turnover rate among the dancers, and they didn't get to know each other intimately.

This particular afternoon, however, they were discussing family and some of the more private thoughts concerning those close to them. The conversation was at a level where they were discussing the gifts that they had chosen for parents, young nieces or nephews, and their own young children. In an environment in which one would expect the conversation to be rather cold, harsh, and impersonal, it was surprisingly gentle and warm.

I don't know if it was just the season, or if I had an extremely flawed perception, but I do know that when the Bronco game ended and I left that establishment, I had an entirely different regard for these young women than I'd had when I'd entered.

I retreated the few miles to my hotel room and relaxed for a bit. I had consumed two or three very large mugs of Heineken. I then left for my dinner reservation, and was seated at a small table in an area that provided a good view of the dining room, providing optimum people watching. I have always enjoyed watching people and judging them without the slightest idea of what they do, think, like, or dislike. Since losing Susie, I dined alone frequently, and this practice had become almost an obsession.

I watched people file in for their Christmas Eve celebrations. There were young families, families of several generations, and several couples. It was the couples that tore at my heart. I had experienced a Christmas and two Thanksgivings since Susie's death. Although each gave me a sense of sadness and emptiness, tonight was very different. I suddenly had a series of sensations. First there was a loneliness like I had not experienced before. An outpouring of anger, to know that Susie had to be taken by such a horrible disease and that, if there is a God, he could display such cruelty as evidenced by her suffering, followed this. My mood would then swing to what I now believe was self-pity. Combined, I was experiencing the most grief I had known since her passing. I wept and felt conspicuous.

I recovered my poise, now feeling that probably no one but my server had noticed. I enjoyed my dinner and the balance of the evening, and I retired at the hotel.

The next day, I woke to sunshine and a brighter outlook. On my way, I visited my brother Ron and his wife, Sheila, to wish them a happy Christmas. Then I returned to Pueblo.

Chapter 30

Plan Disrupted

Little else occurred during the holidays. We had met the year-end deadline for disbursing the liquidating trust, and I was now spending little time with the real estate development.

It was a cold winter, and as can happen in Colorado when the intense cold hangs on for an extended period, I had to monitor my rooftop and the rain gutters, to ascertain that ice dams would not build up and cause leaks in the roof. This was rather strenuous work at times, and I was not comfortable dealing with heights, so the trips up and down the ladder were less than pleasant.

In addition to that, my driveway was rather large, and I found myself shoveling much more snow from it than I wanted. My decision to leave Pueblo for points farther south was bolstered. I often told folks that I was about to tie a snow shovel to the roof of my car and then drive south until someone asked me what that thing was. That was where I would settle.

I did get things sorted and organized, and I discarded several things in order to be prepared when the time came to leave. I had made an irreversible decision. The brown and cold of the winter weather and the seemingly endless quest to hook me up with one of the local women were major factors, but I also had developed a fondness for Austin and the Texas lifestyle. I had friends there, and a fresh start in Texas was appealing.

While I was struggling with all of these issues and planning the move, Jim Gibbons called to get an update on my progress with my moving plans. At the end of this discussion he casually mentioned that Gayle had a friend from California join them over the holidays. He and Gayle would like to invite her to join us for dinner one night during my stay in Palm Springs if it would not make me uncomfortable. "She is a retired school teacher, has a hundred foot yacht in San Diego, and is a fox!" He exclaimed. I think that my somewhat disinterested response was, "Oh why not."

About the middle of January, I received an email from Tom, the realtor in Texas. He had attached a link to a site describing a property in Horseshoe Bay. The home had three bedrooms and two baths. It was located on a large lot with large oaks and all-natural landscaping. The front was enhanced with a beautiful stone facade. It was everything I was looking for. Tom had done his job well. I could join the Horseshoe Bay Golf Club, and it was all within the budget I had established for such a move.

I was excited. I immediately called Tom, asked the few questions I had that the website had not answered, and made an appointment to have the property shown. I was to meet John Wilkinson and his group on January 31, and I had plenty of time to make the trip from Austin to Palm Springs, a drive of about 1,200 miles. My enthusiasm mushroomed over the next several days, and the Mustang was road ready.

A day before I was to leave for Austin, I got a call from someone involved with the holding company trust. A situation had arisen that required a meeting to be held on January 27. There was no way

I would be able to attend such a meeting and drive to Austin before heading to Palm Springs. I decided that I would need to reschedule my trip to Austin and either meet Tom on my way back to Colorado, or drive home and then head to Austin for an extended stay.

I called Tom and informed him of the delay. I made him promise to not let that property go under contract without my knowledge.

Over the next two or three days, we accomplished the tasks required to satisfy the needs of the trust. During this time, I contacted Pat Pate, a friend from the country club in Pueblo. Pat also had a home in Lake Havasu City, Arizona, on the Colorado River, and I now had time to stop there to play a round or two of golf. Fortunately, Pat was available at the time I planned to arrive, and we would make arrangements to play one round at his club and another at one of the public courses. I had never been to Lake Havasu City and was excited to check it out. My golf schedule was complete for the entire trip.

I then took the necessary measures to ensure that the Pueblo house was secured and properly prepared for more of those subzero temperatures that had already occurred in eastern Colorado. Satisfied that all was ready, I headed south to embark on my Palm Springs Adventure.

Once again, it was imperative that I avoid inclement weather at subfreezing temperatures. The Mustang was extremely dangerous under icy conditions. The forecast was favorable for me to take a direct route, south to Albuquerque and then catch to I-40 west into Arizona. Fortunately, the weather was perfect for this part of my journey, and I made excellent time. I arrived in Flagstaff, Arizona, at cocktail hour.

Just off the interstate sits an Outback Steakhouse, my favorite place for a nice premium gin on the rocks and a steak with broccoli when I am on the road. They are consistent in their quality and are normally easy to locate. It saves searching for a dinner spot when traveling. I checked into a chain-operated motel next to the restaurant, and after a couple of hours of snappy patter at the bar with strangers, a great meal, and a bit much to drink, I retired.

The next morning, I mapped a route through the familiar Arizona towns of Sedona and Prescott, and the not-so-familiar ones of Congress, Salome, Vicksburg, and Bouse. I finally reached Parker on the Colorado River. I could now take Arizona State Highway 95 north along the river to Lake Havasu City.

The tee time Pat had reserved was around noon, and when I left Flagstaff, I felt that I had allowed more than adequate time to reach the club. So far, I had stayed on schedule. I had roughly forty miles to go and about an hour to get there. *No problem,* I told myself. I lied! For forty miles, there was a caravan of motor homes. The average age of the motor home drivers was estimated at eighty, but the speed of the motor homes was less than a quarter of that. Traffic in both directions was heavy, and the road was winding.

I immediately called Pat on my cell phone (it was legal then) to let him know I might be a bit late. He bumped the time up a half hour, and I continued on. The traffic became stop-and-go. The blood vessels on most parts of my body had surfaced. Soon Pat was calling me to see where I was. I was now about five miles from the club. It still took me fifteen minutes to cover that distance.

We missed our second tee time and had to wait a while before we were able to tee it up. That was probably a good thing because it gave me time to have a beer and reduce my blood pressure. Pat was gracious through the whole thing and acted as if nothing had happened. It turned out to be an enjoyable round, and we were able to complete it before dark. After all, the sun does set quite early around February first, particularly when one ventures farther south.

After golf, we retreated to Pat's home and invited his wife to dinner. It was going to be a while, so I checked into a motel and then set off to the restaurant. It was an inviting establishment and was located directly beneath and to the side of the London Bridge.

The bridge had spanned the Thames River in London from 1831 to 1967, when it had to be replaced to accommodate automobile traffic. Developer Robert McCulloch, who founded Lake Havasu City, purchased the bridge and had it dismantled after numbering each block. It was then shipped to Arizona via the Panama Canal and Long Beach, California. The bridge was reassembled at its current location.

Pat soon arrived to announce that his wife was not feeling too well and would not be joining us. We had a pleasant time and then left for our respective quarters.

The next morning, we played the round that Pat had arranged at the public course. Pat was one of the top players at our country club in Pueblo, and he throttled me both rounds. I licked my wounds, thanked him, and departed for Palm Springs. My route from the river took me back to Parker and to California Highway 62 just across the river. The Colorado River forms most of the border between Arizona and California.

After passing through the California Agricultural Inspection checkpoint and Vidal Junction, I began a ninety-six-mile journey through the desert to Twenty-Nine Palms, the town that is the gateway to the United States Marine Corps Air Ground Combat Center.

Between Vidal Junction and Twenty-Nine Palms, there are no services and no restrooms. It is okay to need a restroom without having access to one on this segment, because you may pass only half a dozen vehicles, and you can stand or squat anywhere without fear of being observed by anything other than lizards or rattlesnakes. I should mention a vulture or two might be looking from high above. For the same reason that one need have no fear of being observed relieving oneself, one should not be cursed with a fuel gauge reading empty.

Twenty-Nine Palms, Joshua Tree, Yucca Valley, and Morongo Valley are the municipalities that represent the populace of the Upper Desert, an area above the Coachella Valley wherein lies Palm Springs, and the other resort cities of the Lower Desert. The Upper Desert provides off-base housing for the marine base, is the gateway to Joshua Tree National Park, is a bedroom community for employees of the resort cities, and is a haven for retirees and snowbirds. This was my first exposure to all of this area, and for a boy who'd just left Pueblo, Colorado, which he considered brown and barren due to the winter and the vegetation's being in its dormant stage, this area, including the ninety-six-mile drive through the desert, gave a whole new meaning to brown and barren. Pueblo was looking pretty good right now!

Chapter 31

Introduction to the Desert

I passed through the Upper Desert without stopping and began the descent into the Coachella Valley. Westbound California Highway 62 ends when it intersects Interstate 10. I reached this point and took an easterly heading on the freeway. I was instantly surrounded by hundreds of windmills—not the kind that Don Quixote would challenge, but those that generate electrical energy. This was by far the largest accumulation of windmills that I had ever observed, and I had passed concentrations in Texas that I thought were astounding. I was so astonished that I had to stop in order to avoid a driving mishap that might imperil others or me.

I finally gathered my wits and continued on my route. I had no familiarity with this area and so had located a chain-operated motel in Indio that was the most reasonably priced. It was located near the freeway and was easy to find. I entered the office and checked in. I asked for directions to nearby restaurants and was given three or four options. I then went to transfer my things to the room. Big surprise. The room was spacious but was aged, and it had a musty odor with which I had a high degree of involuntary spurn. I returned to the office to check on the availability of another, less offensive room, and was told there were none.

I took a deep breath and decided to check out one of the restaurants. The first, just across the street from the motel, was of Mexican cuisine. Upon entering the parking lot, I was greeted by a rundown building with windows that appeared to have never been cleaned. I retreated without exiting the auto.

The others suggested by the motel clerk, were some distance away. I turned southbound on Monroe Street and was instantly in bumper-to-bumper traffic going nowhere. After about twenty minutes, I had progressed about a block. With the flashing lights ahead, it appeared that there was construction ahead of me. Luckily, I had come to a spot where I could make a U-turn.

I returned to the motel, parked in the space in front of my room, grabbed my phone, and dialed the Marriott reservation number on my speed dial. I asked the person answering the phone for information on rooms in the area. At the time, the most accessible hotel from my location was a Courtyard just off the freeway at Cook Street, in Palm Desert. She gave me the direct number for the hotel because she did not have adequate information available to answer my questions, which were local in nature. I contacted the Courtyard, was given directions, made a reservation, and sighed in relief.

I quickly checked out of the musty motel and arrived at my new setting within a few minutes. I was given a lovely room with a balcony overlooking the mountains to the north. Immediately adjacent to the hotel was an Applebee's restaurant and bar. I recall imbibing in a couple of Sapphires on the rocks with a pair of olives in each. I do not remember what I ate, but I know that for me, Applebee's was an oasis in this vast desert.

I finally retired, happy and contented.

The night before, my introduction to this valley was along the freeway, which was not a good visual inaugural event. The view was barren desert, scarred by railroad and industrial development. This morning I awoke and decided to take a long walk. I was at the intersection of Cook Street and Frank Sinatra Drive.

In the lobby, I checked a map and found that rather than a walk around the block, I could do a walk around the mile. The hotel was located on the northeast corner of a one-mile square, bordered by Frank Sinatra Drive, Cook Street, Country Club Drive, and Portola Avenue; each street was one mile from its parallel counterpart. This gave me a four-mile walk without venturing far from the hotel. The walk convinced me that I had not given the area a fair shake the previous night, when I was dealing with the motel issue, the restaurant issue, and the traffic issue in Indio. I had used a number of expletives regarding this God-forsaken desert, and everything it stood for. After all, I had only seen the barren freeway corridor at that point.

This walk took me down lovely landscaped streets bordering gated communities and golf courses, many with water features. There were palm trees everywhere. It was as if I had entered an alternative dimension, and if I avoided the freeway, I could save myself from the evils lurking in that other dimension.

I had the rest of this day to myself because I was not scheduled to meet John Wilkinson and his buddies from Denver until our tee time the next morning. I decided to drive around the many towns that made up this great resort complex, getting my bearings. It suddenly became apparent that everything I had heard about the Palm Springs area was factual. There were golf courses, restaurants, bars, and hotels everywhere. It had a vibrant atmosphere because thousands of people had made the pilgrimage here to play and escape the rigors of winter in the northern climes.

Downtown Palm Springs echoed the architecture and atmosphere of the era for which it was famous, the early to middle twentieth century. With few exceptions, the other cities were more modern in design and ambience. Cities such as Palm Desert, Indian Wells, and La Quinta were incorporated well after Palm Springs, which was incorporated in 1938.

It was time for lunch, and I returned to the hotel. I had been eating in restaurants for many days, and I now felt like doing something different. I asked the person at the front desk to recommend the best sandwich in the valley. Without hesitation, she directed me to Sherman's Delicatessen, which was located about three miles away. I followed her directions, entered the spotlessly clean establishment, and looked at the menu. I quickly found my favorite: liverwurst on sourdough bread. I ordered it with mayonnaise and onions. I grabbed the bag containing my treasure, made a stop for a six-pack of beer, and returned to my room.

Back in Pueblo, it was probably about ten degrees above zero in the sun. Here, I opened a beer and took it and my sandwich to the table, on the balcony, which overlooked those mountains to the north. In the shade, I guessed the temperature to be sixty-five or seventy degrees. The box holding the sandwich seemed to weigh in at around five pounds, maybe a little less. I had assumed that inside that box were containers of condiments, and maybe French fries, which I had asked them to hold. I opened the box and jumped back. There looking up at me were about four inches of layered slices of liverwurst. They were tucked between two slices of extremely fresh sourdough bread, with plenty of mayo and onion. I was in liverwurst heaven! It took me about an hour to finish that monster sandwich, along with the two beers with which I coaxed it down.

All of this time, I was enjoying the view and the warmth. I was trying to imagine what it must be like back in Pueblo, but my mind would have no part of those thoughts, and I dozed off.

I toured the area a bit more, walked in and out of some of the nearby attractions, and then rested and watched some television. I recently had used the TV little other than for local news, but now it was a welcomed change of pace. It was mostly mindless entertainment, but I also did watch a local newscast to pick up some flavor of the area.

My several miles of walking during the day must have burned the fuel that I had consumed at lunch quickly because I was hungry once again. On my morning walk, I had passed a Morton's the Steakhouse and decided to give it a go; I had not patronized one in some time. I parked a decent distance from the restaurant (one must keep moving, you know) and made my way to the front entrance.

There were three women approaching the door as I arrived. I opened it and held it for them. These ladies were not old enough to be my mother, I don't think, but I was sixty-five, and they appeared to outdate me by a decade or more. Two of them looked me over from top to bottom and said something like, "What are you doing out here alone? Maybe you should come join us so that you will be safe." I was somewhat taken aback, but I graciously declined the offer, shooed them into the restaurant, and allowed the door to close behind them. Visions of some of my suitors from Pueblo had quickly come to mind, and my automatic escape mechanism had been triggered. I decided to choose another location in which to dine, and I returned to Applebee's.

The following morning, it was time to meet John and his contingent from Denver. I was told that we were playing at the Marriott in Palm Desert. I had passed a Marriott on my morning walk the day before and thought that I was in good shape, time wise, because it was quite close to the Courtyard from which I had just checked out. I arrived at the pro shop, where they were unable to find the reservation. The person assisting me excused himself, got on the phone, and returned with some slightly disturbing news. The reservation was at the Marriott Shadow Ridge Resort, which was about three miles away. I was at the J. W. Marriott Desert Springs Resort. I rapidly reloaded my things and hustled the three miles to find John waiting in the parking lot. With his help, I was able to put myself together in time to just make the tee time. Never assume!

John's two friends were a delight to be around, and the four of us enjoyed a great day of golf. These people had been to the area before and had made dinner plans for the evenings that we would be together. One of John's friends had procured another friend's vacation home at no charge in the Chaparral Country Club, a short distance from where I had been staying. There were supposed to have been two bedrooms, with two beds in each room. Unfortunately, that was the case in only one of the bedrooms. We unloaded our luggage, freshened up, and then went to our first prime steakhouse, located in La Quinta, LG's. It was somewhat of a feast, and after a rather long day and the drinks that we had put away, we headed back to the house.

I immediately offered to sleep on the couch, because John and I were assigned to the bedroom with only one bed. He offered some resistance but soon acquiesced, and we all turned in. I don't recall any particular noises, flashes of light, lumps in the couch, or strange critters under my sheets, but I did not sleep the entire night. Upon arising in the morning, the first thing on my docket was to make a reservation back at the Courtyard for the balance of my stay.

For the next four days, we ate too much, drank too much, played a ton of golf, and pretty much fulfilled all of the requirements of a group of over-the-hill men on a golfing holiday. We maybe fell a little short in the bragging department. It was a humble group.

On Saturday evening, I received a call from Jim Gibbons, who invited me to Gayle's father's home in Rancho Mirage to watch the Super Bowl the next day. Gayle's father is a retired dentist who had acquired the nickname Doc somewhere along the way, and he was celebrating his eightieth birthday the next day—the reason that they had all gathered. I was playing the last round of golf with the boys from Denver in the morning, and I would have sufficient time to freshen up and join them in the afternoon. I accepted.

Chapter 32

Puzzling Acquaintance

Sunday morning, February 4, 2007, began as the other days on this golf outing had: breakfast at the Chaparral's Restaurant, and then off to the golf course. I believe I managed a score in the mid-eighties, which for me was quite good at that stage of my not-so-successful golfing career. After we had finished, I had lunch with the Denverites and bid them farewell. Their flight home left later that evening.

I managed to get showered and drive to Lake Mirage, a lovely gated community that catered to the tennis crowd with at least a dozen courts, as well as two meandering lakes that provided a lakefront site for every home in the complex. I arrived just shortly before kickoff. As I approached the parking area for Doc's townhome, I noticed a black Mustang convertible parked there. It was somewhat of a magnet for my auto, and I parked alongside it.

I crossed the street with a rather lively step and pressed the doorbell button. I waited. Then I pressed the doorbell button once again. Finally, the door opened, and there before me stood a stranger. She reached out with her right hand and said, "Hi, I'm Shari!"

I engaged her outstretched hand in a gentle but firm manner, and I was countered with a firm grasp and an enthusiastic handshake. I responded simply, "I'm Harvey."

Something clicked inside of me. There was an alluring way about this young woman. She was obviously somewhat younger than I, was very attractive, and radiated a warmth that I did not recall having experienced before. I had no idea who she was, and because she had introduced herself to me, no one offered more information as the evening progressed. Was a she relative? Someone's wife? A neighbor? I was intrigued but was careful. *Remember, Harv, you have no interest in anything that might begin a new relationship!*

Before I had arrived, Shari had apparently attempted to activate the widescreen television in the living room and found it to be nonfunctional. It seemed that everyone in the place had then tried to revive it, to no avail. Shari took much teasing for the remainder of the evening for "destroying" the television set, and we retired to the master bedroom to view the game. Most of the guests sat on the large bed, and the rest occupied the two or three chairs that would fit in the room.

Shari now seemed rather reserved, which was strange, because she had been quite the opposite when she had opened the door and greeted me. She sat on the opposite side of the room from me, and although the atmosphere was friendly, there was little conversation between us.

We ate, drank, and cheered whatever team that Jim preferred. As a Denver Broncos fan, I had little interest in the outcome unless the Broncos were involved. The Chicago Bears and the Indianapolis Colts were the contenders. I had no interest in the Colts, and I don't believe anyone else did. The Bears, on the other hand, were in the same division as Jim's Detroit Lions, and therefore we cheered the Lions on.

I must admit that I had difficulty taking my eyes off Shari. There was something about this young lady that intrigued me. She was lovely to look at and seemed refined and stylish in an unassuming way. Her eyes and smile were captivating. She willingly absorbed the abuse she was taking over the TV, which indicated a charming sense of humor. Who was she?

When the game ended and it was time to leave, Jim and Gayle cornered Shari and me in the kitchen and asked if we could join them for dinner on the following Tuesday. That was it! Shari was the girl who was to join us for dinner during my stay. It all fell into place: it was a trap!

I quickly agreed and asked when and where. Then to my delight, Shari responded positively while flashing that smile in my direction. We both wished Doc a happy birthday. When I turned for the door to leave, Shari sidled up to me, took me by the right arm, gave a bit of a squeeze, looked into my eyes, and bid the others good night as we slipped through the door. My heart skipped a beat. A sensation resembling a low voltage electrical shock pulsed up and down my spine.

I asked which car was hers, to which she replied, "That black Mustang convertible next to the pretty blue one."

She asked what I was driving, and I remarked, "The pretty blue one." We both were driving Mustang convertibles.

I opened the door for her and bid her good night. I returned to my room at the Courtyard and sat on the bed, staring at the floor. I was thinking that I had suddenly become confused. I had taken a solemn vow to avoid another relationship for fear of once again experiencing the pain I had endured with Susie's suffering and my loss of her. Now, a new acquaintance had emerged, and I eagerly anticipated seeing her again. I knew virtually nothing about this person, yet she had my mind focused on her. There was definitely a physical attraction, but also something more in the warm and exhilarating sensation that coursed through me when she touched me. When she spoke, her voice had a similar effect. I could not get her out of my mind, although admittedly I was not trying very hard.

First, I thought that going ahead with dinner on Tuesday could be a very dangerous move on my part. I had so far avoided any possibility of becoming entangled in a liaison that might lead to commitment, or worse, any feeling of guilt. After all, it had been only two years since Susie's passing. The next morning, I could easily tell them that I must return to Pueblo immediately for business reasons, and that I would be unable to join them for the planned dinner.

After much thought, I decided that my plan was a cowardly retreat. I would go to dinner with the three of them. If I were to remain somewhat aloof while being cordial, I could then avoid disappointing Jim and Gayle, excuse myself reasonably early, and head back to Colorado early the following morning. The perfect plan.

My mind was barking instructions, but my heart was not listening.

Jim and I spent both Monday and Tuesday on the valley's exceptional golf courses. On Tuesday evening, the four of us convened at the Cedar Creek Inn on South Palm Canyon Drive. After we had been seated for a bit, I realized that I had left my reading glasses in the Mustang and excused myself to retrieve them. As I emerged from my chair, Shari also stood and suggested that she could use a little fresh air. We walked to the car together, and it occurred to me that this lovely woman whom I barely knew seemed to enjoy being with me. I was having unexpected feelings of my own toward her. I sort of felt as though I were back in my teenage years and dealing with some form of infatuation. I am not certain, but I believe that during the return to the restaurant, she once again took me by the arm, and I felt a chill run through my spine.

Although my thought process was monopolized by Shari, I could not help but momentarily divert to the amazing chopped Cobb Salad that had been placed before me. This salad was formed as if it were packed into a large bowl and then turned upside down on a plate with the bowl gently removed, revealing a dome shaped mass of greens, bacon, egg, avocado, chicken, onion, blue cheese crumbles, and whatever else they found in the kitchen; it was finely chopped and held together with a thick ranch dressing. It was an amazing work of art and was quite sufficient as a dinner for one who had developed an enormous appetite after a day of golf.

We enjoyed the dining experience and each other's company to the extent that the decision by the group was made to extend the evening by having an after-dinner drink at a nearby restaurant and lounge that Shari remembered as being cozy with an outside patio and large fireplace. We proceeded to Europa, which was about a mile from the Cedar Creek Inn.

Europa is a small, very romantic restaurant located in the Villa Royale, a quaint resort in the south part of town. It is reportedly the former villa of the famed Norwegian Olympic figure skater and film star Sonja Henie. One enters the facility via a narrow passage that borders a large fountain and the entrance to the lobby before opening into the main courtyard that harbors a large swimming pool and very attractive desert landscaping. Across the courtyard from the lobby is the entrance to the restaurant, and the dining patio extends to the left of that entrance. After dark, the lighted plants, the pool, and the fireplace contributed to an intimate mood that well suited our group.

We entered the bar area through the restaurant entrance and were greeted by Matt, the bartender. He guided us to the patio, ignited the fire for us, and then took our drink order. He was soon back carrying a tray filled with brimming vessels. It was a beautiful evening, and with the fireplace, the snappy patter, and some additional alcohol, it magnified my attraction to Shari. During the conversation, it was evident that this venue was one of her favorites.

The evening was pleasant. We were all good friends and had many narratives to reveal about one another. It seemed as if it would last forever, but it did come to an end. As we were saying our goodbyes, I got Shari a short distance from the others and apprehensively asked if we could have dinner on Thursday evening. She indicated that she had other plans for that evening, but she would see if they could be changed. I gave her my number, feigned going to the men's room, and quietly made a reservation in the dining room for dinner on Thursday. When I returned, we exited the restaurant.

We made small talk while gazing into one another's eyes as she entered her Mustang and prepared to leave. Rather than that longing look of two people who have a deep emotional connection, the gaze seemed riddled with question marks for both of us. What was happening here? We bid each other good night, and I watched her Mustang leave the parking lot.

I could not believe what I had done. I had sprung the trap that I had feared for the past two years. Not only was I experiencing feelings toward this charming girl, but I was the one pursuing her, or at least it appeared that way to me. What if we should become close, and she should become ill or have an accident? I didn't believe that I could again watch someone for whom I had close feelings suffer. I had set the stage, and I could only hope that she would be busy on Thursday so that I could leave the next morning.

I have no idea what I did that evening. I may have had a drink somewhere on my way back to the hotel, or I may have returned and gone to bed. I only know that since losing Susie, I had taken a hardened approach to any possible future relationship. My rulebook was now in jeopardy.

I spent the following day, Wednesday, exploring the Palm Springs area. Although I had been in the area for the past several days, my range of circulation had been limited to the hotel, nearby restaurants, golf courses, and those locations where I had spent time with Jim, Gayle, and Shari. There was much more to this valley that I had overlooked. There are seven cities that border California Highway 111 and that represent the resort portion of the valley. They also embrace the approximately 130 golf courses that occupy this 25-mile corridor. Each of these cities boasts its own history, culture, and identity, of which there is plenty distributed throughout.

Probably the most fascinating aspect of the area is its colorful history, from the well-known days of the Hollywood icons in the forties, fifties, and sixties to the lesser-known tales of the local Indian tribes and the pioneers who settled here. Another fascinating part of the local history is the colossal training base for General Patton's legions, as well as his presence in the area. I spent most of the day getting my bearings for navigating the valley. Deep down, I had a feeling that this was not going to be my last trip to the area.

Late in the day, I received a call from Shari. She said that she had been able to free herself for Thursday, and we could go forward with dinner plans. My heart jumped right into my throat and out of my mouth. After returning my heart to its rightful location, I accepted my feelings of delight, regained my composure, and offered to pick Shari up at her home in Paradise Springs for our trip into Europa. She quickly accepted and provided directions.

I was due in Pueblo on the weekend, and it was necessary that I call and delay my arrival until the first of the week. I was now free to leave on Friday or Saturday and arrive home in time to meet my committed schedule.

Chapter 33

Attraction to Enchantment

Thursday is somewhat of a blur in my mind. I am pretty certain that I played golf in the morning, but beyond that, I remember nothing until it was time to leave for Shari's home.

My mind was racing because the casual acquaintance that had seemed to develop over the past few days had now become more formal. I found myself truly looking forward to seeing Shari. There was something tearing at me that I could not deny. I was thoroughly perplexed. I felt my barriers crumbling around me, and I was helpless. I had all of those plans to move to Texas, a thing that I was truly anticipating with enthusiasm. Now I could feel a tug of war coming on with myself.

I was unfamiliar with the route to Shari's subdivision. Relying on my photographic memory, I remembered her saying something about Palm Drive as the interchange on which to exit the I-10. It was now dark, and a highway sign appeared indicating that Date Palm Drive was the next exit. Well, it had the words Palm Drive in it, so I took the exit. I followed her directions and turned right onto Date Palm Drive, which by those directions should have taken me about four miles to a traffic signal, at which I was to hang a left. Unfortunately, it took me about two miles, and the road ended at a three-way stop. I had to turn right or left. Since my next turn via her instructions was left, I chose that. Now I was on a very lightly traveled two-lane road with no lighting, in the middle of nowhere. We had a reservation at a place that was small and very popular, which meant if one was too late, it could negate the experience. I decided that, against my better judgment, I should call Shari and see if a navigational adjustment was in order. (Men never need directions, you know!) It turned out that Palm Drive was correct, and that if I traveled another couple of miles, I would intersect it. I thought, *She will now think that I do not listen, and she will become wary. Or she will excuse my confusion and think my being humble enough to ask for directions is worthy of praise.*

I made it to her delightful three-bedroom home in a very new, small, age-restricted, gated community, which was appropriately tagged Paradise Springs. When she opened the door, once again her girlish charm overwhelmed me, and a strange sensation swept through me. We both stood there, warmly smiling at each other. *What a beautiful smile,* I thought. She asked me in to see her home. I was captivated by the magnificent view of the valley lights below. What a sight! She gave me a quick tour because she was very proud of this new home, into which she had moved just a short time before. It was beautifully decorated. Time was running short, and we had to depart.

We arrived a little early at Europa. This allowed us to take a seat at the bar, where Matt the bartender queried about our order. That prompted us to inquire about the wines. He offered a sample of the Buehler Zinfandel that, after the traditional wine tasting ritual, proved to be quite pleasing to both of us. That ritual is wasted on the likes of me, because legs, bouquet, and those other strange measures of greatness have nothing to do with the effect of that delightful solution coursing over my taste buds. We ordered two glasses and perused the menu as we waited, sipping the very pleasing Zinfandel.

Shari was leaning toward a seafood pasta dish, and I eyed a seafood casserole that sounded more like a lot of shellfish in a decadent cheese sauce. Soon we were led to our table for two, which was small and located in an intimate wing of the main dining room, directly across the wing from a fireplace that was glowing cozily.

We ordered another glass of wine. The server brought delectable bread and a small aperitif. We visited for a while, mostly conversing about our backgrounds, families, and current life situations. Shari was so easy to talk to, and I felt as if I had been in her company for years. We then summoned the server and ordered the dishes that we had previously chosen. He disappeared.

Then it happened!

A few minutes following our submitting our dinner order, something came over me, and I placed both hands in the center of the table. This one small act would change the rest of my life. My hands were palm up, in an obvious gesture for her to take them. She did without hesitation, and we once again gazed into each other's eyes. This time there were no question marks. The most pleasing sensation I have ever known took control of my senses, while at the same instant an amazing emptiness occupied my stomach—in a good way. I wanted to laugh and cry simultaneously. I am certain that I was shaking. I was as helpless as I have ever known. All I wanted to do was hold this woman.

Fortunately for me, Shari experienced the same phenomenon. She did have the composure to insert a bit of levity into the moment by reaching across the table, lightly touching my nose, and declaring with a mischievous sort of smile, "You're so cute!"

I am sure that I smiled, blushed, and replied, "I may be cute, but you are absolutely beautiful." If I didn't say it, I certainly felt it.

As we looked softly into each other's eyes, there was no need for words. We once again joined hands, and once again a flush of warmth surged through me as chills played up and down my spine. I had no time to think of my longstanding vow of aloofness toward interactions with another woman. I murmured, "What just happened?"

Shari firmly squeezed my hands, which amplified the mysterious sensation I was experiencing. She softly stated, "I'm not sure."

Our server approached with two plates and set them before us. The presentation was fantastic, and the aroma of the sauces was delectable. The problem was my appetite had left the building. I was going to be unable to eat, and I revealed such rather bluntly. Shari indicated that she was dealing with the same issue, adding that maybe we should ask for take-away containers. We did so.

We sat looking at each other, smiling, talking little and somewhat nervously, and sipping what remained of the wine. The server delivered the containers, I covered the check, and we stepped out through the front entryway into a new world for both of us. While standing near the pool, I set the bag holding the containers on a patio table, turned to Shari, and took her into my arms. We stood holding each other firmly for some time. I released her slightly, looked deeply into her eyes, and whispered, "I really like you."

She whispered back, "I really like you too."

We proceeded across the courtyard to leave the Villa Royale, and as we approached the large fountain, I once again turned Shari toward me, gently took her into my arms, and placed my lips onto hers. Her lips were soft and inviting. We held each other tightly as we experienced a bonding that neither had expected at the beginning of the evening.

I have little recollection of what followed. We may have stopped for a cocktail somewhere before returning to Shari's home. I do know that she asked if I would be interested in riding the Palm Springs Aerial Tram to its upper terminal on Mt. San Jacinto the following day. My answer was a resounding yes. I do remember that we kissed once again at her doorstep as I was leaving. This time the kiss was more of a statement than a question.

Chapter 34

Euphoric Twenty-four Hours

The balance of that evening, I had a lot going on within that sphere above my neckline. I had a little something in my room that contained alcohol, which helped settle me a bit. I felt excitement about what was occurring. For two years, I had locked out all possibility of becoming attached to another woman. In a matter of a few hours, all barriers had been eliminated with absolutely no input from me. I was suddenly obsessed with this woman. I was in fast forward and had no thoughts of turning back.

In our conversations, Shari had revealed that she had been separated from her former husband for some time, and that her divorce was final a few months earlier. She had also retired from thirty years of teaching just days before our meeting. This young lady had experienced two life-changing experiences very recently, and I was sure she did not intend to settle for one of the first hombres to ride into town. I decided that the best thing for both of us was for me to avoid scaring her off.

I picked her up the next day, and we headed up the aerial tram. This was some amazing ride. The gondolas on the tram carry many passengers and rotate 360 degrees as they ascend or descend between the lower and upper terminals. One gets an eerie feeling of moving from stark desert environment to an alpine situation in a matter of ten minutes. It may be 70 degrees on the desert floor less than 500 feet above sea level, but only 30 degrees at the upper terminal at an elevation of just over 8500 feet. The scenery is spectacular in all directions, and the rotating gondola provides everyone on board with a live slideshow as the car moves from one environment to another.

Once on solid ground at the top, we strolled through the upper terminal to view the two restaurants and the U-shaped bar, all of which provide enchanting views of the pine trees just outside the building, or the desert floor below along with the mountain range on the far side of the valley.

We then walked down a steep winding ramp to the forest floor, and there was snow. I had just come from where I had played golf, and now we were romping in snow! It was not like Colorado snow, but snow nonetheless. As with all desert natives, Shari becomes enamored whenever there is snow in sight, or particularly when there is snow underfoot. For me, at this time of year, after several months of winter, snow is somewhat of an annoyance. Her company offset any possible aggravation, and I thoroughly enjoyed being with her as a little girl's joy streamed from that adorable face.

The chronology of the next hour or so escapes me. The next item on the agenda was to return up that arduous ramp to the level of the upper terminal building. It is winding, and one would swear that it gains two feet in elevation for very step forward. Believe me, there were a ton of steps forward. Having come from the higher elevations of Colorado, I weathered the exertion better than Shari, who was accustomed to an elevation about eight thousand feet lower. Even so, my lungs began to burn by the time we covered the relatively short distance.

I know that we did have a beer, or maybe a wine, or maybe more at the bar. I also vividly remember our strolling out onto the balcony that faced the desert floor. It was chilly and breezy on that veranda, which caused her to inch closer and closer to me until I embraced her rather tightly to protect her from the nipping breath of the wind. My vow of bachelorhood was in serious jeopardy.

I think this was about the time that I suggested I might make a few calls, rearrange my schedule back in Colorado, and stay a few more days. Shari came to her senses first, and using a very sensitive approach, she suggested that it would probably be best if we took it a little more slowly. I suddenly remembered the conversation I'd had with myself regarding the first hombre to ride into town, and I agreed with inward reluctance. Shari had broken a date with a person she had encountered on an internet-dating site to spend more time with me, but I did not want to monopolize her time, which could prove to be distasteful to her at this stage of her life.

We rode the tramway back to the lower terminal and headed toward Paradise Springs. She had promised to treat me to the world's best hamburger at a place near the interstate, next door to the Harley Davidson dealer. This place was appropriately billed The Handle Bar. I believe that at this moment, we both felt, and in our separate ways hoped, that a long-term relationship might be brewing.

We did stop at the Handle Bar. We were nearly the only people in the place, which at best had the atmosphere of an auto repair garage, with bar-height, round, stainless steel (I think it was stainless) tables on a concrete floor; painted concrete walls; and ceiling tiles whose original color was fully obscured by a combination of grease from the vents and old cigarette smoke.

What happened next changed the place into a warm, inviting room that I would yearn to return to until its apparent economic demise a few years later. A woman about forty years old approached our table. She was an attractive blonde with a few tattoos, and she had a voice that, although definitely feminine, had an authority about it that would challenge a drill instructor from a special forces training camp. We were in a dive bar, and it probably required a person of authority to keep the peace. This woman proved to have a most unique and captivating sense of humor, and soon we each had a mug of thirty-degree, fresh, draft beer sitting before us. She took our order for the famous ten-ounce cheeseburger, and within a few minutes, she returned to the table to converse while the kitchen prepared our order. She kept us laughing until a bell from the kitchen signaled that our meal was ready.

Miss Congeniality set a basket before each of us. The contents were simple: one gargantuan cheeseburger and a helping and a half of onion rings each. The burger was touted as being ten ounces, and if I were to accuse the place of false advertising, it would be for understating the size and cholesterol content of that burger. I was facing the biggest culinary challenge of my life, consuming the entire contents of that basket without experiencing cardiac arrest or having to burn my shirt afterward. The thing oozed melted cheese and drooled a consistent stream of delightful grease with each bite. In what seemed like the hour it took to devour that masterpiece, I must have filled a landfill with napkins used to wipe the grease from my chin, to avoid having my shirt appear as if I had just changed the oil on an eighteen-wheeler. Never have I had a burger experience like that.

On the infrequent occasions that I set the cheeseburger down, I sampled the onion rings, which added another dimension of guilt to the experience. All of that, washed down with the ice-cold draft beer, created a memory that is indelibly etched in my mind for the rest of my life, and possibly longer. I think the entire bill for both of us did not exceed twenty dollars.

Throughout this experience, I was mesmerized by the wit and charm of Shari. It was obvious that with this extremely casual adventure, we had become very comfortable with each other. My mind was no longer occupied with thoughts of doing or saying the right thing—I was being myself with no pretensions. I had a very strong feeling that the same transition had taken place with Shari.

During the drive from the Handle Bar to her home, we began talking of real things in our lives. They were more intimate things, such as our previous marriages, what our expectations of the future were, and our relationships with family and friends. We were rapidly becoming confidants. At this point, I did not want to head home. I guess I was afraid that if I left, it might be the end of this amazing episode in my life.

I accompanied Shari to her door, and after some small talk, a kiss or two, and possibly a tear in my eye, we parted. She was firm that I was banned from the desert for at least thirty days. I know that she was having a similar tug-of-war over our parting, but good sense dictated that we take a breather and think this thing through.

Chapter 35

Two Hearts Pass in the Night

I stayed in my hotel that night and then began the trek back to Pueblo the following morning. I had fourteen or fifteen hours of driving ahead of me, which allowed plenty of time for reflection and self-analysis. I imagined dropping everything in Colorado and moving one thousand miles away. What about my family, my friends, and the resulting support group that now was a phone call away, or at worst a two-hour drive?

My business career in Pueblo had left me with a network of resources that I would abandon if I pursued this relationship. Medical, dental, legal, accounting, my favorite restaurants, my banking relationships, my mechanic—it seemed an endless list. A move such as this was like beginning my life all over. But wait! Wasn't I about to move to a golfing mecca just outside of Austin, Texas? I had already made the decision to begin a new life. Now I had a particularly attractive option—maybe!

I knew that if Shari and I were to develop an intimate relationship, it would involve my moving to California. She was not prepared to desert her close family ties, particularly her aging mother and her two grown children, with whom she had an enviable bond. I would never ask her to make such a sacrifice. My parents had both passed on, and I had no children.

I caught myself having these kinds of thoughts after knowing this person for less than a week. How adolescent. How wonderful to have these feelings at my age.

On the return trip, I had decided to stay over one night in Gallup, New Mexico. Gallup is a town of about twenty thousand, located on the far western edge of the state. It provides a point almost halfway from Palm Springs to Pueblo. I wanted an early start the next morning, and I quickly unpacked the car and found a restaurant for an early dinner. I returned to the room and, with some apprehension, made a quick call to let Shari know that I had arrived safely. I am pretty certain that she had asked me to do that. We talked for longer than I had intended, primarily recounting our adventures of the past several days and letting each other know how enjoyable those moments were.

This practice of cell phone communication would become a twice-a-day event until my reappearance in California. It is indelibly noted that Shari's mother, whom I was yet to meet, invariably asked this question whenever Shari was with her during one of our calls. "What the hell do you two have to talk about that could take that long?"

My return to Pueblo was a bit of a disappointment. It was still cold. Everything was brown. I wrapped myself in completing the final phases of the holding company trust because I felt a strong sense of obligation, but knew that unless Shari extended that thirty-day ban to something more permanent, I would be returning to the California desert in a relatively short time. I had to complete that trust's functions before returning.

Late on February 13, I suddenly remembered that the next day was Valentine's Day. For two years, I had not dealt with things of a romantic nature. I had to swing into action. Shari and I had discussed our musical preferences, and it was obvious that she was touched by both song lyrics and melodies. There was a particular song of the country crooner Don Williams that I felt very closely defined my feelings toward Shari. Purely by accident, I happened to have acquired an extra album of his with that particular song included. I rushed to a nearby drug store, found an appropriate card, quickly authored some profound romantic lines, dropped in a small box of Enstrom's Almond Toffee, and overnighted my Valentine's Day offering to Shari. I then had a couple of drinks and some dinner, watched some television, and went to bed.

The next morning, I got up, had a cup of coffee and was immediately overcome with a remorseful bout of anxiety. What if she received my package and felt that I have moved too quickly? It could be another adolescent move that had a strong potential of frightening her away. Where did I keep coming up with these silly notions? For the balance of the day, I worked on some of the trust follow-up, with recurring dread of the possible results of my unretractable overnight package.

In the late afternoon, I was sitting in my office and still working on those trust issues when the doorbell rang repeatedly. I jumped from my chair, proceeded to the door, and opened it to face a Fed Ex driver holding a letter-sized package. The return address was Shariann Alexander in Desert Hot Springs, California. My heart joyously sprang into my throat. With disbelief, I opened the overnighted envelope to find a CD and a Valentine's Day card enclosed. The note in the card referred me to her favorite song on the Celtic Woman album she had sent. Although we both knew of the other's favorite types of music and some of the artists, we had never discussed swapping albums. Neither of us had any indication that the other was sending that package. I thought this must be some form of prophecy.

The next few days were difficult because I now longed to see Shari again. Partly because she was so intriguing in so many different ways, partly because I had so enjoyed her company, and partly to confirm that the initial magic we had both sensed in the beginning remained following this seemingly endless separation.

The days passed rather quickly. I was concentrating on two things: fulfilling my business obligations, and preparing for the return trip to California. Suddenly the time to return arrived. Although we had continued the twice-a-day phone calls throughout my banishment from California, I was desperate to gaze into those beautiful eyes and hold that delightful woman in my arms.

During our frequent phone conversations, Shari had informed me that on the day I had chosen to arrive in the Coachella Valley, and for a few days after, she would have one of her sorority sisters and her husband visiting her. She therefore requested that I stay in Desert Hot Springs so that I would be nearby, and I could join them for a meal or two and possibly a cocktail. She was anxious for us to meet.

I was happy to accommodate and was pleased that she wanted me to be interrogated by one of her closest friends. I was not at all familiar with the Desert Hot Springs area, and I asked if she could pick a suitable location. She knew of a spa resort hotel on the main artery through town, where friends had stayed many years before, and which they had apparently enjoyed. Thus began the exposure to my own personal hovel.

Chapter 36

The Leap

Let us track back a bit. I finally left Pueblo and was bound for Southern California. It was important that I take a route different from my previous trip because I did not know how many times I might make this journey in the future, and I did not want the drive through Arizona to become mundane. I chose to travel to Grand Junction for my first night's stay. I had dinner with an old friend and co-worker from my Aspen days, and his wife; they had retired to Grand Junction. It was an enjoyable, happy hour type of evening. Fortunately, it ended early, and I was able to get a good rest and hit the road early.

It was about 750 miles from Grand Junction to the California desert, and I chose to spend the night in St. George, Utah. Although Susie and I had spent some time there on the golf courses, we had done little to explore the area. Since her death, walking about five miles a day had become a habit for me. I had been somewhat bound to the car seat and a bar stool the day before, and so I hoped that I would find a suitable trail near St. George.

Find it, I did. On a road north of the city is the Snow Canyon State Park. This canyon was formed by quartzite sand blown over the area almost two hundred million years ago. The resulting dunes, which could be almost two miles thick, hardened into sandstone. Over the many centuries since, weather erosion and volcanic activity have shaped this beautiful arid landscape. Towering red cliffs, whispering sand dunes, and layers of black lava on off-white sandstone provide a mesmerizing backdrop to the clear blue sky and myriad of plant life that abound in the area.

Through the canyon winds a paved pedestrian and bicycle path that allows virtually all who desire the opportunity to enjoy this breathtaking, pictorial experience while realizing a good dose of healthful outdoor exercise.

After a glass or two of wine and a small steak at Texas Roadhouse, I retired. The next morning, I arose early and made my way to the park, left my Mustang in the parking area just outside the gate, and proceeded on my five-mile, round-trip walk. The rising sun on the amazing rock formations, along with the exhilaration provided by the brisk morning air, caused me to stop and realize just how much I appreciated all that I had, as well as the opportunity given me to be in this spot, at this time. How many people in this world must rise today and be faced with hard labor, stressful corporate politics, hunger, or political strife? Yet I was here, able to witness the grandeur of this moment. I was near the top of the list of the luckiest people in the world.

Right then, my phone rang; it was Shari. My heart gave me an extra beat, and the chills ran up my spine, as had happened each time she touched me or when I first heard her voice. We went through our "good morning" ritual and then made the final plans for my arrival at the Hot Springs resort, where she had made reservations for me that evening.

It was now about seven thirty, and I did my morning prep before getting back on the road. I needed about six hours of driving time and was headed for some freeway traffic in the San Bernardino area that could become congested at times. I was able to depart St. George around nine, which should get me into Desert Hot Springs just after 3:00 p.m.

The drive was uneventful, with the exception of an accident in Redlands that caused a brief delay. Soon I was nearing Desert Hot Springs. Shari had indicated that she would meet me at the hotel, and she would check me in with the desk. I called to let her know that I was nearing the place, and I was informed that she was in the room, waiting my arrival. I experienced the excitement of a high school boy on his very first date who had somehow arranged a date with the girl desired by every other boy in school. She was the prom queen and cheerleader. It was similar to the dog that caught the car it had been chasing and suddenly was faced with a dilemma: "What do I do now?"

I had been steadfast in my vow to not enter another caring relationship. Before I'd met Shari and spent time with her, I had felt my oath was safe. All that I needed to do was not return, and I could go forward as I had planned. Now, I was returning with a new anticipation as to where this rendezvous might lead. Was I ready to face the risk of allowing myself to become vulnerable, to the extent that I'd follow my heart and let this woman enter it, if she was so inclined? I had to remember that—God forbid—I could be faced with another heartbreaking loss.

I called her mobile number, and she answered instantly. She was in the room awaiting my arrival. I followed her instructions and soon found myself approaching a rather weathered, gray-looking building that was two stories high. There was parking reserved for registrations, of which I took advantage, and I entered through double-glass doors sadly needing repair.

Once inside, it was as if I had entered a bat cave—and not the one housing the headquarters of the famed Caped Crusader. This was a cave lined with concrete, which my memory appropriately described as dark and dingy, with more than a hint of mildew odor. One might expect to be wading through bat guano on the way to the registration desk. The place was apparently designed to meet the whims of guests of a past era of which I had no recollection. It had long ago passed its peak, and now there was little being done to maintain the property.

I notified the desk of my arrival, and a friendly person there gave directions to the room. The room was on the second floor, and I climbed the stairway. Once there, I followed the breezeway around about half of the interior of the building. In so doing, I could not help but notice the pool and its surroundings below. A group of several small, jetted pools that were undoubtedly filled with the waters of the hot springs for which the town was named embraced the main pool. Also, throughout the pool area were scattered several thatch-roofed gazebo structures for protection from the sun. Judging from the several very large, very white bodies lounging around the pool, it was obvious that there was need for a great deal of shade. I saw none of the Hollywood types, normally pictured in hot spring resort ads, lounging at this pool. The thatching material appeared as if there had been no repair or replacement for several decades, and the obvious white splotches of missing pool liner, made me a little suspect of the establishment.

I approached the room with my heart welled up in my throat, and I tapped on the door. It opened almost immediately. There before me was the most beautiful woman I had ever seen. She was wearing a nicely fitting pair of white pants with an also nicely fitting orange top that I will never forget. It offset an incredibly attractive face wearing the prettiest smile in all of California—and it was directed squarely at me. I was overcome by those chills that she so easily inflicted on me. We embraced, tightly. Then came the kisses. We might have spoken before those physical things; I don't recall. We then entered the room, where Shari had champagne and strawberries waiting. Now, I am not a champagne drinker, but that was the most delicious liquid refreshment in my memory. The strawberries were very large and very sweet. We hugged and kissed again and again, and then we lay on the bed and visited for a long time. We were both avoiding saying the frightening "L" word, however I do think that we both felt it. Although the physical surroundings were something less than romantic, this rendezvous had invigorated my desire to be near this amazing woman.

Until now, this had been a romance borne of my loneliness, the new surroundings, and the adventuresome atmosphere that the Palm Springs area radiates during the winter months. This extraordinarily attractive, interesting, and clever woman of course accentuated all of this. I felt as if I were traveling through a romantic movie from the fifties or sixties.

It was now that I began a serious inward struggle with myself. I had pledged that I would remain single for the balance of my life in order that I might not suffer another dark period such as that which had resulted from watching the suffering and agony that Susie had endured with that hideous disease called cancer. All of that, coupled with the heartbreak I had experienced and continue to experience from her loss, had resulted in my erection of a virtual stonewall between any future commitment and me.

Shari had conveyed a message of a strong attraction to me, as I had also conveyed to her. I felt a commitment was going to be necessary if I wanted this connection to continue, because she had intimated that her plans for the future included remarrying. I could not believe the depth of the feelings that I had for Shari. I lay awake nights during this time, wondering whether I could release myself from this self-imposed exile to the extent that I could support my half of a wholesome relationship. My little battles sometimes lasted for hours.

My plans before meeting Shari included the projected move to Texas, which would allow me to escape the sometimes-brutal winters of Colorado while also dodging the social pressures in Pueblo, which had driven me to a nearly reclusive existence. Although this plan would most likely have replicated that type of existence, in my mind, I perceived only the bright sunshine, wildflowers, and fresh-cut grass without considering the possibility of high humidity, tornados, annoying bugs, scorpions, and the other things that one faces in the South. In short, my vision for the future in Texas was of an extremely happy loner, content with playing golf, taking long walks, drinking probably more than one should, cooking for myself, and watching a great deal of television.

Now, as I compared that existence to the possibility of a life with Shari here in the desert, it began to look somewhat bleak. Although we had known each other for a rather brief period, when I laid these two scenarios side by side, I had real problems considering a life without Shari.

Chapter 37

Unspoken Commitment

The next few days were somewhat of a whirlwind. I spent only two nights in this hot springs resort because I began to find things in the room that were less than sanitary. The folks who I had observed on my arrival were the cream of the crop. When I made my trek from the room to the office, a number of residents who did not include the word hygiene in their vocabulary passed me. The crowning blow was about 1:00 a.m. during my second night in the room. Two women in an adjoining room began arguing. Soon it turned into an all-out shouting match with their either throwing things at each other or throwing each other; I could not tell which. Without fanfare, I checked out the next morning as quickly as possible. Shari and I both refer to the place as the hovel to this day.

I did find another resort hotel just across the street, which turned out to be quite satisfactory. I resided there for the next two nights.

As noted earlier, Shari's sorority sister Annette and her husband, Dan, were staying with her during this period. I was invited to dinner to meet them. Although I was focused on nothing but Shari at the time, we enjoyed each other's company and have experienced an enduring friendship since.

After Dan and Annette departed, Shari invited me to leave the hotel and stay with her. My acceptance took a nanosecond. From this point forward, we spent virtually every minute together. I moved into a hotel once more to accommodate Shari's daughter, who visited from Santa Barbara sometime during this period.

We hiked, explored the local restaurants and brewpubs, traveled to Laguna Beach (on Shari's nickel), and spent many a night drinking wine and contemplating satellites from the lounge chairs in Shari's backyard.

We learned about everything that there was to know about each other. We agreed to be totally open and honest with one another, and I do not believe that we left a stone unturned. Shari even shared her book that she had structured from an online dating site, which spelled out everything that she was looking for in a companion. I was hesitant at first to expose myself to this information, but I was pleasantly surprised to find that I would need little tweaking in all categories except one: religion. She was a churchgoer, however she was not devout. I never attend church. It was a minor issue.

Chapter 38

Meeting Family

Shari decided it was time for me to meet her mother, Ann Alexander. Although I knew that her approval was not necessary, it was always a bit uncomfortable to be set on that stage, when a mother must acknowledge that she would share her daughter with a man she had never met, even at our age. We picked up Ann at her home and carted her off to her favorite Chinese restaurant, just south of downtown Palm Springs.

Ann was a person who spoke plainly—if she thought it, she stated it. One never needed to be concerned about one's status with Ann. She was short and slight, but it was obvious that she was in charge of any situation at her discretion.

We had a pleasant conversation, enhanced by the fact that the restaurant was very short of clientele that evening. There was little background noise to interfere, and the people serving us, with broken English, did not hover in lengthy dialogue. I found it easy to be with Ann and Shari together, and we discussed many things, but mostly we focused on my background and plans for the future.

Ann did share some of her experiences with her husband, who had passed away less than a year before. Her husband, Bill, had been the band director at the famed Chi Chi Club in Palm Springs. This was a supper club with live entertainment, much of which was people of big name stature who stopped at the club on their way from Los Angeles to Las Vegas. It was a place to warm up for their acts in Sin City. He had become friends with many of the stars and had provided accompaniment to people such as Bob Hope, Lena Horne, Sammy Davis Jr., Louis Armstrong, Nat King Cole, Red Skelton, Liberace, and others. The club operated from the forties into the seventies, the peak of Palm Springs' reputation as the getaway of the Hollywood elite; it was a very interesting time for Shari and her family. Bill has a star on the Palm Springs Walk of Stars.

We spent a couple of hours visiting, and then it was time to return to Ann's home. I parked in the driveway, and we walked her to the door. She and Shari exchanged hugs and kisses, and then Ann turned to me. She looked me straight in the eye and bluntly stated, "You're neat!" I could not have scripted a better compliment. I truly felt that I was part of the family at that point, and it was the beginning of a close friendship that lasted until Ann's death in May 2009.

Ann owned a boat that was moored at a slip in the Marriott Marina in downtown San Diego. Shari would drive her mother to the boat for at least one long weekend a month. After I had been around for a while, I was invited to join them on occasion, and during these trips, we would stroll on the San Diego Bay Walk through Seaport Village. It was a great time for people watching and sampling a myriad of food and beer, all while observing the abundant marine activity on the bay itself. Sometimes we three would walk together, and sometimes it was only with Shari. These are some of my fondest memories of time spent with Ann, and although sleeping accommodations on the boat were "cramped-comfortable," they were some of my most enjoyable times.

I met Shari's daughter, Jennifer; her son, JW; and her brother, Dennis, as various events brought us together. We formed excellent bonds through our love for Shari, and we have enjoyed celebrating many occasions together, several on that boat in San Diego with the entire family.

In April 2007, we traveled to Colorado so that Shari might become acquainted with my home there. Shari had been raised in the desert, and she had very little experience with snow. She was delighted when we awoke one morning and found it snowing outside.

During this trip, Shari, being the good sport that she is, was introduced to many of my friends. The first was a cocktail party with about twenty folks who were primarily former associates at the bank and former customers. The second was a retirement party thrown at the Abbey of the Holy Cross, in Canon City, Colorado, by Dan Tanner, a former holding company associate and member of the board of directors of Centennial Bank. At this party were colleagues from my bank examining days, customers of Centennial Bank, former directors of the bank, former bank employees, and many friends from Pueblo and Canon City.

There were smaller and less formal gatherings. In particular, the two more intimate gatherings were where Shari met Stan Herman at a dinner in his home, and where she met Roy and Lynetta Gillmore in a delightful restaurant just outside of their hometown of Westcliff.

During this same trip, we journeyed to Denver, and I introduced Shari to my brother Ron; his wife, Sheila; and their son and daughter. We also got her acquainted with my brother Sam, my sister Carolyn, and Carolyn's daughters. Shari would meet my siblings from Nebraska, Gordon and Kathy, along with their spouses and children later.

Harvey Hoff

This was a whirlwind trip for us, but it was a particularly stressful one for Shari because she was encountering my friends and family at a hurried pace. I was fortunate to be meeting her friends and family in the desert one at a time over several months. We felt that it was important to both of us that we arrange these introductions, because we had spoken of many of these folks with each other, and it was more meaningful if one could put a face with a name in such conversations. Besides, it was always helpful to learn more of people through their friends.

We also realized that in both of our social circles, there was a great deal of curiosity about the person each of us was considering for a lifetime commitment.

Chapter 39

The Big Question

In April, Shari and I traipsed up the Ernie Maxwell Trail outside of Idyllwild, a small mountain community about an hour's drive from the desert. Shari's lifelong friend Pauline Costi, who lived in Idyllwild, had urged us to make the trip. She had not met me, and of course she was cast under the spell of curiosity along with all of the others. The four-mile, round-trip alpine setting of this trail was reminiscent of my mountain days in Colorado, and it would become one of our most frequented hikes over the next few years. This was probably the beginning of our addiction to hiking, which has taken us over numerous states, the European continent, and hundreds of miles on foot.

In May, Shari introduced me to the Joshua Tree National Park. I had no previous knowledge of the place and had no expectations. We entered the park from one of the less traveled access points, and the road led us through a recently burned area. For some distance, all that remained were the charred skeletons of these rare trees. Once we passed through that area and had reached the trailhead, I found that no picture of this landscape I might have fabricated in my mind could have equaled the beauty, serenity, and mystique of the park.

The area that we negotiated for about six miles harbored the largest of these phenomenal desert plants, the tallest of which can reach heights of forty feet. That is the height of the tallest in this 550,000-acre park; there could be taller specimens in other unmonitored locations. The Joshua trees resemble a patio umbrella with a slim, rather gangly trunk for a pole, and a yucca plant splayed at the top in the place of the umbrella itself. After a winter of plentiful moisture, the trees will blossom with clusters of large waxy, white flowers that are unlike anything I had previously observed.

We spent a few hours in the park witnessing the many geological formations, a good number of which are giant smooth boulders, some seemingly as tall as a five- or six-story building. These stones are clustered in arroyos and may appear in deeper canyons and sometimes along the rims of high cliffs. It makes for a very interesting visual experience, as well as a physical challenge while attempting to navigate the slippery devils during an ascent or descent of one of the many washes incorporated into the more difficult portions of the trails.

The vistas from many points of the park will feature stunning panoramas of the nearby mountain ranges. In the spring, following a winter bountiful with moisture, the peaks will display snowcaps, which provide a magnificent contrast to the desert sands below. The endless variety of plant life can maintain a stark beauty in this inhospitable environment; they all seem to flourish where precipitation is scarce, and summer temperatures reach well over one hundred degrees.

We found ourselves spending time in San Diego, enjoying the boat and the bay walk along Seaport Village, and truly getting to know one another in the limited living area that the craft provided.

We also began spending the after-dinner hours reclining on the two large, comfortable lounges in Shari's backyard. We spent hours sipping that Buehler Zinfandel, to which we somewhat attributed those magical moments at the Europa Restaurant and thus this newfound, exhilarating relationship. The time passed quickly on these evenings as we spent the hours searching for man-made satellites drifting through the late-evening, crystal-clear skies, counting them for recording in our cerebral scrapbook. I believe the most observed in any one night was thirteen.

After breakfast one morning, I was sitting at the bistro table in the kitchen, and Shari was standing nearby. I could hold it in no longer. I looked into her eyes and stated, "I love you!"

She immediately approached, held me tightly, and softly replied, "Oh, I love you too!" We had avoided this at the beginning, but now it was an obvious and amazing thing.

Shortly after and without formality, we mutually agreed to get married. Shari had quickly become my best friend, and I became hers. Any thoughts of my remaining alone or relocating to Texas were now behind me. We had both divulged our most personal thoughts and issues to each other, and for both of us, there were no concerns of past or future events that could create a division between us.

Early in May, I took Shari to Gottschalks, a department store in Palm Springs, where she chose a simple band adorned with delightful glimmering emeralds and diamond chips, for her engagement and wedding ring. A few days would be required to have the ring fitted, and when it was completed, I picked it up on one of my trips into Palm Springs. Upon arriving home, I extracted the ring from its white, velvet-lined, red ring box. I had Shari sit on the couch in the living room, kneeled between the cocktail table and the couch, and said, "Will you marry me?" She responded with an instant beaming smile and a resounding yes. We were now officially engaged.

We met on February 4, 2007, and agreed that a wedding day exactly six months later would be appropriate. I was now spending virtually 100 percent of my time in California. After discussing both sides of the issue of housing, it was determined that because Shari's children and her mother were domiciled in California, and because I had no close personal ties to Colorado, it would be fitting that we make our residence in California, in Shari's house.

Chapter 40

It's Official!

In June Shari and I returned to Colorado and made arrangements for some of the furniture from my home, which I had previously listed. It would prove to be a logistical nightmare. Although Susie and I had not completely furnished my home, many items would not fit in Shari's house. Most notably, my rather fancy treadmill, the bigger-than-life chess table, the large TV, my china hutch, a heated recliner with massage capability, the Spinet piano, and several other noteworthy items.

Some of these I sold to friends who were familiar with the items, and they laid claim the minute I announced I was moving. Some were worn enough that I felt obliged to make them available to the Salvation Army, which sent its large truck and gladly retrieved the large assortment that I had placed in the driveway. The balance were miraculously disposed of through the generosity of Roy Gillmore, who graciously hauled them to his wife's gift/antique/tack shop in Westcliff, Colorado, a small mountain community west of Pueblo. Some of the items Roy and Lynetta purchased themselves, and the balance they sold from their shop, refusing the commission I offered. I think they were quite happy to have me exit the area.

July was a whirlwind of activity, most notably Shari's preparing for the wedding on August 4 and my frantically tying up the loose ends in Colorado. The month is somewhat of a blur, but I have no doubt that the one certainty is that we consumed rather vast volumes of that Buehler Zinfandel during the period.

Finally, the day of the wedding arrived. Shari is a very creative person and has a penchant for things of hearts, roses, and glitter. Our modest, outdoor ceremony lacked in none of these. The two of us spent a great deal of time prior to the ceremony decorating the arbor with tulling, roses, and lights. It was August in the Southern California desert— the temperature was 118 degrees! I am from Colorado and am used to mild days and cool nights. I sweat profusely if the temperature exceeds 80. I was going to be married outside at 118. Was this a test?

The venue was the Wedding Chapel, a courtyard surrounded by La Plaza, a historical shopping area of Spanish architecture located in downtown Palm Springs. The pastor was a rather jovial-looking fellow with a fitting personality. He was efficient and helpful in guiding us to the ceremony that we had envisioned, which was quite simple and to the point. The vows that were made during the ceremony, though short, were very special and meaningful to us.

The ceremony took place at twilight with guests numbering fewer than thirty. They were seated on both sides of the aisle with friends of the bride on one side and friends of the groom on the other. Because the groom's side boasted only two members, Stan Herman and John Harris, the other guests dispersed among the vacant seats to avoid embarrassment to the groom.

There were red roses covering the arch and white rose pedals scattered down the aisle. Shari had a beautiful wedding dress that exemplified her lovely features and her gregarious personality. Each time I looked her way, my heart leapt into my throat, and that's the truth!

Don Williams's song *Till the Rivers All Run Dry* was playing on the pastor's boom box at the rear of the seating area. The song had become a favorite of ours since I had shared that album with her on Valentine's Day. Shari and I gathered with the pastor under the arbor. The ceremony began with the words from that song, the beginning of which was, *Till the rivers all run dry, Till the sun falls from the sky, Till life on earth is through, I'll be needing you.* These words perfectly described our feelings for each other.

Following his brief opening words, Shari and I exchanged our vows, which were also shorter than most. He then pronounced us husband and wife. We kissed a kiss that sent a surge of passionate commitment through me. Throughout the past six months, as Shari and I became friends, lovers, and finally committed partners, I never felt a bit of apprehension. At this moment, although I was swept by a feeling of wonderment and pride to be the husband of this wonderful person, I also embraced the reality that just now, I had begun a new and wonderful chapter in my life. This beginning, with my relocating to California, with my loving dedication to Shari, and with my leaving Colorado and my friends and family, was the formal beginning.

Somehow, someone had managed to light all of the two-foot-long sparklers that Shari had procured for this moment. We left the altar and traveled back down the aisle through a tunnel of blazing fireworks as the entire group of guests held those magnificent pyrotechnics over our heads. As we exited, another Don William's song, *I Believe in You,* followed us out.

Prior to this day, I had met a sparse few of Shari's friends, along with her immediate family. Today I met additional friends, cousins, and her Aunt Mary, who is one of the most interesting people I have known. With this new collection of friends and acquaintances, my new life began. I would dine, drink, and share my new wife with them, and they with me. Some of us would travel together, some would become partners in family business transactions, some would pass on, and some would find new partners in life. However, that night we would all gather at the Europa Restaurant and celebrate Shari's and my joining the rest of our lives.

The entire assemblage now moved the mile or so from La Plaza in downtown Palm Springs to the Europa Restaurant on east Palm Canyon Drive. We were greeted warmly by the manager and the executive chef. Cocktails were provided from the ample inventory in the lounge, and we had ordered the now highly regarded Buehler Zinfandel along with another favorite that Matt the bartender, now Matt the restaurant manager, had introduced us to: St. Francis Chardonnay. People were mingling as they did at these things. Shari delighted in having her friends and family together in one place, and I enjoyed the opportunity to become acquainted with them all.

It was the beginning of a wonderful festivity, and things were going as we had planned. Suddenly and without warning, the lights went out. Now, I am not afraid of the dark, but when it was 118 degrees out, and the air-conditioning fails in the middle of our party with a few octogenarians attending, I panicked! Someone took credit for this calamity, claiming that she had mentioned Shari's ex's name the instant before it had occurred. I tend to believe that it was the age of the building and an electrical system that needed a serious upgrade.

We waited several seconds for the usual situation, where a circuit breaker on the power company's grid is tripped and resets after fifteen or twenty seconds. This is when the power is generally restored. It was not in the cards this evening. The power remained off, and calls to the utility confirmed that it was not on their system. The problem was internal.

Shari's brother, Dennis, is a contractor, and the husband of one of the cousins was an electrician. They exhausted their combined books of knowledge but were unable to locate the disruptive cause. We then turned to the management for suggestions, and after a time, we determined that the show must go on.

The entire restaurant staff rose to the occasion. With battery-powered lights (the natural gas and water were still functioning), they proceeded. The meal preparation took somewhat longer than anticipated, and during the waiting period, our bar and wine bill soared with the mercury in the thermometer. One of the sorority sisters circulated among the guests with iced towels to place upon sweating necks. Somewhere during all of this, a toast was offered by my two now well-oiled friends. Back in the kitchen, the entire team rotated in and out of the inferno to accomplish the task at hand. They had not even a fan to assist in cooling that small area with the ovens and cooktops blazing. The only means of cooling off was to step outside into the triple-digit heat. It was an enormous effort. The result was an exceptional meal, with all of the elegance and attention to detail that we had previously experienced in the restaurant. It was thoroughly enjoyed by everyone.

The most frightening part of the evening for me occurred just before the cutting of the cake. Shari's sorority sisters lined up for their traditional embarrass-the-new-husband dance, and then they sang their traditional embarrass-the-new-husband song, "Come Say You'll Be My True Love." Immediately following that, one of the girls informed me that this was a tightly knit group, and that a man did not marry just one of them, but the entire group. Just what every groom wants to hear! It turned to be more of a family of friends situation than a polygamous one.

It was now time to cut the cake, which Shari had designed with the help of Pastry Swan Bakery in Palm Desert. It was small, only three layers of chocolate cake with chocolate mousse and topped with chocolate fondant. It was pretty to look at, topped by a crystal heart-shaped loop with a single crystal heart dangling in the center. It was, without exception, the most amazing cake I have ever experienced, particularly with Shariann force-feeding me.

Following the cake-cutting ceremony, most of the entourage moved on to Melvyn's at the Ingleside Inn in Palm Springs. There in the lounge played an experienced piano man, circa the Sinatra era. He played enough of the old hits from the forties to sixties to fill even my voluminous appetite for such music: the Chairman of the Board, Dino, and Tony Bennett, along with a seemingly endless list of memories. The man played, the people danced, and a magnificent time was had by all. In some cases, it was too magnificent.

Shari and I retreated to our suite at the Villa Royale. The next morning, we rose to have breakfast with some of the wedding guests who had stayed at the inn. We said our goodbyes and returned to the room, and there we lounged and relaxed for a couple of days. It had been an evening of excess consumption by any measure, and it had been a long and exhausting six months. The relaxation was a necessity.

We then returned to our home in Desert Hot Springs. It was the official beginning of our life together. The partying and celebration had ended. Now was the movement forward of two people who had, under two very different circumstances, found their lives transformed—both tragically, and both having been left with nothing more than a question mark about the future. Shari had chosen to take the path that our meeting had provided. On the other hand, I had been determined to move in an altogether different direction, to two "-nesses," selfness and loneliness, all due to my fear of another tragic end to someone I loved. Shari's determination to meet a person that one of her friends had suggested, and my willingness to appease her friend by agreeing to have one dinner with them, moved us to a path of togetherness, friendship, and love.

Epilogue

It has been a decade since Shari and I met. I wrote this book for two reasons. The first is, that reliving the past ten years through creating this manuscript has allowed me to enjoy one of the most amazing periods of my life, as if I were experiencing it once again in real-time. We have become the closest of friends while relishing in a loving bond. This bond is one of the very special ones. Although we do have disagreements from time to time, they are short-lived and are resolved through our amazing ability to compromise. In fact, Shari's mom often exclaimed, "Don't you two ever argue?"

Shari and I have traveled extensively, mostly on the roadways of the Western United States, but we have also visited Canada, Alaska, Hawaii, and Europe. We have spent our summers on the Oregon Coast, which we consider one of the most beautiful and underrated places on our continent. We have been on both ocean and river cruises, flown in float planes, taken dinner trips on historic railroad routes, climbed ancient volcanoes, trekked through a two-mile lava tube, taken Dungeness crab from the ocean, observed a multitude of whales, summered on the banks of the Madison River in Montana, and hiked up inclines for which we were ill prepared. At times, we also drank more wine than two people have a right to drink. We have experienced all of these adventures and look forward to many more.

I often reflect on what might have been if I had closed my heart to this amazing woman. Just before meeting her, I was dead set on moving from a comfortable situation in Pueblo, Colorado, to Austin, Texas, where I would have been living in old memories and trying to resurrect old friendships. The only person in the area that I had remained in close contact with was John Harris, and he was travelling extensively. He would have been in Austin rather infrequently, and on those occasions, he would have had family occupying his time.

I was not seeking a new life—I was running from the memories of the previous one. I fear now that the consequences of that flight may have shortened my life significantly, because I would undoubtedly have left the many caring and supportive friends in Pueblo, and I would have found myself very much a recluse in Texas. It was a time of floundering for me, and I was not making good decisions.

The choice of a lifetime was made for me. Thinking I was doing my friend Jim Gibbons a favor by agreeing to meet his girlfriend's sorority sister for one dinner, I stumbled onto the most important event since losing my wife Susie. The armor with which I had shielded myself from another broken heart was shattered. With no input from me, I began a new life.

The second reason I wrote this book was to encourage others. I feel that many people have suffered a loss such as mine, and they proceed in life without the love and companionship that I have found. Many experience feelings of guilt, fear of deserting those deep feelings that had been shared with a passed spouse, or concern with the ability to meet and become close to another person. These folks may live through a possibly shortened existence without the happiness and desire for life that a new loving relationship can offer.

My own mother, who was widowed at the age of forty-six, never remarried. I often wonder how different her life might have been had she agreed to accept some of the offers she had to meet someone. To my knowledge, she never did.

The fear of another tragedy in my life was not the only concern that I had. I knew that my life with Susie and my feelings for her could not end with her passing. How could another woman be comfortable knowing that? I was very open with Shari about the possibility that I might stumble and call her by Susie's name, and that I was frequently dreaming of Susie when Shari and I met. Shari's strong love for me has alleviated this issue. She has established a comfort level for me in this regard that has resolved any concerns about its interfering with our relationship.

To that extent, Shari has insisted that we hang a portrait of Susie and me in the hallway with her family pictures. She has displayed horse paintings treasured by Susie, and she has hung many of Susie's original watercolors throughout our home.

Susie had urged me to find another companion after she was gone. Shari's and my discussing that openly, and my fully understanding her feelings about it, preclude any possibility of guilt in that regard.

The depth of my love for Shari has mitigated those fears of heartbreak and sorrow, which I fought after Susie's death, throughout Shari's and my meeting, and the entire time we were building our relationship. I discovered that to truly love a person, one must be able to set such issues aside. I have done that successfully.

Shari and I have developed a stress-free relationship through our rituals of hugging and kissing morning and night. We never retire in the evening or begin a new day without expressing our appreciation for each other. We keep our relationship interesting through experiencing travel, different types of music, cooking and developing new recipes together, watching old sitcoms, and searching for innovations in our restaurant adventures.

Our love and respect for each other continues to grow as the years pass.

If our story can be an inspiration to just one person who can break away from the grip of fear and guilt following the loss of a companion, then the time spent writing this book will be well rewarded.